Homo Natura

Incitements

Visit the series web page at: edinburghuniversitypress.com/series/incite

Homo Natura

Nietzsche, Philosophical Anthropology and Biopolitics

Vanessa Lemm

EDINBURGH
University Press

Edinburgh University Press is one of the leading university presses in the UK. We publish academic books and journals in our selected subject areas across the humanities and social sciences, combining cutting-edge scholarship with high editorial and production values to produce academic works of lasting importance. For more information visit our website: edinburghuniversitypress.com

Edinburgh University Press Ltd
The Tun – Holyrood Road, 12(2f) Jackson's Entry, Edinburgh EH8 8PJ

Typeset in 11/14 Bembo by
IDSUK (Dataconnection) Ltd, and
printed and bound in Great Britain

A CIP record for this book is available from the British Library

ISBN 978 1 4744 6671 4 (hardback)
ISBN 978 1 4744 6673 8 (webready PDF)
ISBN 978 1 4744 6672 1 (paperback)
ISBN 978 1 4744 6674 5 (epub)

Erudite and provocative, this book breathes new life into Nietzsche's insight that there is no essence to human beings, other than their capacity for transformation, metamorphosis and becoming. Replacing the binary opposition of nature to culture with a dynamic continuum, Nietzsche challenges us to think differently about what it means to be human. Lemm argues forcefully for Nietzsche's inspirational role in contemporary debates on new materialism, posthumanism and the renaturalisation of philosophy. An illuminating and timely intervention.

Rosi Braidotti, Utrecht University

In *Homo Natura* Vanessa Lemm delves into Nietzsche's enigmatic, and often misunderstood, exhortation 'to place the human back among the animals'. With rigorous scholarship and original analysis, Lemm brings us to an understanding of what 'naturalism' this is: not one advancing a biological reductionism. To the contrary, it finds in nature a principle of creativity and generativity that carries a surplus of life over any existing order, so that in returning to nature the human can exceed itself. Among its many merits, Lemm's reinterpretation of the body in Nietzsche's posthumanism offers a provocative reading of the centrality of gender and sexuality to the most radical aspects of his thinking. *Homo Natura* is a key text for those interested in what Nietzsche's philosophy can offer for contemporary feminism and Anthropocene thought.

Brian Massumi, author of *99 Theses for the Revaluation of Value: A Postcapitalist Manifesto*

This book offers what may well be the finest appreciation to date of Nietzsche's relation to philosophical anthropology. It is certainly the most provocative. Lemm makes a strong case for reading Nietzsche as a thinker of the historicity of human nature, and in so doing she mounts an important challenge to simple-minded naturalistic and positivistic appreciations of him. The book abounds in fresh insights and suggests new and novel directions for thinking. It will appeal to anyone with an interest in the contemporary pertinence of Nietzsche's modes of thinking, as well as in issues concerning biopolitics and in the possibilities of posthumanist thinking.

Keith Ansell-Pearson, Professor of Philosophy, University of Warwick

Lemm's book is highly original and makes a stunning contribution to contemporary Nietzsche scholarship. In fact, the book shows how Nietzsche's influence on contemporary philosophy goes far beyond what others have imagined. This is a must read for anyone serious about understanding Nietzsche's thought and his legacy.

Kelly Oliver, Vanderbilt University

Contents

Acknowledgements

This book is dedicated to my wonderful children, Lou, Esteban, Alizé and Sebastian. They are the inspiration of my life. I am deeply indebted to my life companion, Miguel Vatter, and thank him for commenting on multiple iterations of the book manuscript. I am extremely grateful for their support.

Sections of this book have been presented at numerous conferences and seminars. I particularly appreciate the questions and feedback received from audiences at the Colloque International Nietzsche et la religion, 5–6 April 2019, Sorbonne-Université, Paris, France; the Jahrestagung der Nietzsche Gesellschaft, 'Geschichte und Gedächtnis', 11–14 October 2018, Nietzsche-Dokumentationszentrum Naumburg, Germany; the Silser Nietzsche-Kolloquium 'Wahrheit und Lüge', 27–30 September 2018, Sils Maria, Switzerland; the Friedrich Nietzsche Society Annual International Conference, 'Nietzsche and the Politics of Difference', 20–21 September 2018, Newcastle University, United Kingdom; and the International Conference Nietzsches Anthropologie, 12–14 July 2017, at the University of Erfurt, Germany, generously funded by the Thyssen Foundation. Chapter 1, 'Kantianism, Naturalism and Philosophical Anthropology', is an expanded and significantly revised version of 'Who is

Nietzsche's *Homo Natura*? Self-Knowledge, Probity and the Metamorphoses of the Human Being in *Beyond Good and Evil* 230', *Internationales Jarhbuch für Philosophische Anthropologie* (2018): 33–49. Chapter 2, 'Humanism beyond Anthropocentrism', is an expanded and significantly revised version of 'Friedrich Nietzsche on Human Nature: Between Philosophical Anthropology and Animal Studies', in Brian Massumi and Molly Hand (eds), *Animals and Animality in Literary Studies*, Cambridge Critical Concepts Series, Cambridge: Cambridge University Press, 2018, pp. 197–214. An earlier version of Chapter 3, 'Psychoanalysis and the Deconstruction of Human Nature', has been published as 'Deconstructing Human Nature: Ludwig Binswanger on *Homo Natura* in Nietzsche and Freud', in Daniel Conway (ed.), *Nietzsche and The Antichrist: Religion, Politics and Culture in Late Modernity*, London: Bloomsbury, 2019, pp. 205–27. I thank De Gruyter, Cambridge University Press and Bloomsbury for their permission to use these materials.

Abbreviations

References to Nietzsche's unpublished writings are standardised, whenever possible, to refer to the most accessible edition of Nietzsche's notebooks and publications, *Kritische Studienausgabe* (KSA), compiled under the general editorship of Giorgio Colli and Mazzino Montinari. In the cases in which the KSA are cited, references provide the volume number followed by the relevant fragment number and any relevant aphorism (for example, KSA 10:12[1].37 refers to Volume 10 fragment 12[1] aphorism 37). The following abbreviations are used for citations of Nietzsche's writings:

A   *The Antichrist*
AOM   *Assorted Opinions and Maxims*
BGE   *Beyond Good and Evil*
BT   *The Birth of Tragedy*
CW   *The Case of Wagner*
D   *Daybreak / Dawn*
EH   *Ecce Homo* (sections abbreviated 'Wise', 'Clever', 'Books', 'Destiny'; abbreviations for these titles discussed in books are indicated instead of Books where relevant)
GM   *On the Genealogy of Morals*

GS	*The Gay Science*
HC	*Homer's Contest*
HH	*Human, All Too Human*
HL	*On the Use and Disadvantages of History for Life*
KSA	*Kritische Studienausgabe* (my translation)
SE	*Schopenhauer as Educator*
TI	*Twilight of the Idols* (sections abbreviated 'Maxims', 'Socrates', 'Reason', 'World', 'Morality', 'Errors', 'Improvers', 'Germans', 'Skirmishes', 'Ancients', 'Hammer')
TL	*On Truth and Lies in an Extra-Moral Sense*
UM	*Untimely Meditations* (when referenced as a whole)
WS	*The Wanderer and His Shadow*
Z	*Thus Spoke Zarathustra* (references to Z list the part number and the chapter title followed by the relevant section number when applicable)

How can we think the de-humanised (entmenschte) *human being when the human being is the de-animalised* (entthierte) *animal?* (KSA 9:2[45])

Introduction: Who Is Nietzsche's Homo Natura?

Immanuel Kant inaugurated the age of the human sciences by placing above his famous three questions, 'What can I know?', 'What ought I do?', 'What can I hope for?', the overarching question: 'What is the human being?' (Kant 1912: 343). Michel Foucault concluded his critique of the human sciences by announcing 'the imminence of the death of the human being' (Foucault 1994b: 342). In between, and preparing the way from one to the other, stands Friedrich Nietzsche's famous aphorism 230 of *Beyond Good and Evil: Prelude to a Philosophy of the Future*, in which Nietzsche offers an answer to Kant's question by introducing the enigmatic term *homo natura*.[1] For Kant, the human being was the lawgiver for nature. Thus, his question asks about the pragmatic conditions for a rational natural being to raise itself above nature in complete freedom. By contrast, throughout his writing career Nietzsche insists on the continuity between nature and the human being, and on the impossibility of attaining a transcendental standpoint outside of nature. However, this does not mean that Nietzsche erases 'the human being' in some sort of ontological monism. Rather, this book argues that *homo natura* stands for the paradoxical formula in which the human is caught in a movement whereby the more natural it is, the more overhuman it becomes.

1

In this movement, embracing the human being's more 'natural naturalness' (HL 10) leads to an overcoming of the human that is oriented towards the becoming of the overhuman.

It is difficult to overstate the importance of the aphorisms related to *homo natura* in the development of Nietzsche studies during the first two decades of the twenty-first century. There is hardly a more contested interpretative terrain than the debate over the meaning of *homo natura* and related terms such as nature, naturalness, renaturalisation (*Vernatürlichung*) and their significance for Nietzsche's thought as a whole. Nietzsche's naturalism has recently and insistently been compared with Charles Darwin's evolutionary paradigm (Leiter 2013; Emden 2014; Richardson 2009). On this view, natural history means the history of the biological evolution of forms of life. But far from subjecting the human species to the same laws of evolution that apply to all other living species, the expression *homo natura* is employed by Nietzsche to mark the distinction between what is natural and what is decadent or counternature in the human species as a living species. Not everything achieved by the human species should be valued as a successful adaptation to circumstances, just like not everything that happens can be judged as to its rightness or truth in accordance to a pre-given, rational standard.

But in what sense is nature or *homo natura* a standard or measure to judge the worthiness of human life? Nietzsche presents the attainment of *homo natura* as the 'strange and insane task (*seltsame und tolle Aufgabe*)' to 'retranslate (*zurückübersetzen*) the human being back into nature' (BGE 230). Today, the human sciences inaugurated by Kant have enthusiastically taken up Nietzsche's task by embracing the Darwinist revolution and taking an evolutionary turn in the hope of producing empirically testable hypotheses to explain the manifestations of human life.

2

In its evolutionary and behaviouralist forms, naturalism is all the rage in the human sciences and, more recently, in philosophy.

Homo Natura: *Nietzsche, Philosophical Anthropology and Biopolitics* offers a new interpretation of Nietzsche's idea of *homo natura* as an answer to Kant's question that seeks to avoid reductive or scientistic naturalism. For Nietzsche, the task to retranslate human beings back to nature is to be carried out by scientists (*Erkennende*). However, these scientists must also be distinguished by their probity (*Redlichkeit*) and courage to face the 'terrible basic text of *homo natura (schreckliche Grundtext homo natura)*' (BGE 230). This book attempts to probe this terrifying basic text that qualifies human life. The central hypothesis is that nature's basic text is terrifying to the extent that it contains what is unknowable and undiscoverable by a positivist conception of science, something about nature that is 'beyond good and evil' and that, when acknowledged by human life, transforms this life into something creative and thus worthy of affirmation.

In aphorism 14 of *The Antichrist*, Nietzsche announces that he has 'changed (*umgelernt*)' his way of thinking about human nature and that he has 'placed the human being back among (*zurückgestellt*) the animals' (A 14).[2] This book argues that the discovery of *homo natura* does not lead Nietzsche to discard history and to adopt a scientific conception of biological evolution that replaces it. Rather, the renaturalisation of the human being goes hand in hand with a renaturalisation of history. Nietzsche asks what difference the discovery of *homo natura* makes for our historical self-understanding. What does the 'return to nature' and the renaturalisation of the human being mean for our understanding of history? I offer two possible answers to this question: first, it allows us to write a natural history based on the human body. Second, such a natural history reveals a conception of human nature that is essentially engaged in cultural (self-) transformation, and as such overcomes the dichotomy between culture and nature.

Since the key to *homo natura* lies in establishing a relationship with what is unknowable, the truthful scientist committed to probity envisaged by Nietzsche must be able to pose the question of '"why have knowledge at all (*warum überhaupt Erkenntnis*)?"' (BGE 230). In this sense, they must scientifically call into question science itself. This book argues that Nietzsche's desideratum may have been fulfilled, at least in part, only after his death. Nietzsche's call to renaturalise the human being is here understood as a call to future thinkers to conceive new and revolutionary answers to address the human need to give meaning to life, or to lead a meaningful life, and its intrinsic failings.

Arguably, several thinkers developed discourses after Nietzsche as a response to the perspective on naturalism and life expressed by his term *homo natura*: philosophical anthropology, Freudian psychoanalysis, gender studies, biopolitics and posthumanism are among the better known ones. This book approximates an answer to the question of the meaning of Nietzsche's naturalism through an engagement with these discourses, insofar as they thematise their debts to Nietzsche's motif of *homo natura*. What ties Nietzsche's *homo natura* to all the above is the production of a knowledge of human beings that transforms them from being objects of theory to being subjects of a truth-telling practice, no matter how terrible this truth turns out to be.

Chapter 1, 'Kantianism, Naturalism and Philosophical Anthropology', tracks the shift from Kant's transcendental founding of anthropology to Nietzsche's reflections on *homo natura*. Contemporary discussions have largely been dominated by accounts of *homo natura* that revolve around the question of Nietzsche's relation to the life sciences in the nineteenth century, especially the spread of Darwinism. One of the common assumptions in this literature is that Nietzsche had the opportunity to break from Kantianism by adopting the new perspective of the life sciences. Brian Leiter is one of the most radical proponents of such a scientistic interpretation of *homo natura*. For Leiter, Nietzsche's naturalism consists in identifying the human being as a natural organism whose natural attributes can be accessed and causally explained through the empirical natural sciences. Leiter employs the formula *homo natura* to debunk continental readings of Nietzsche that seek to turn the real world into a text that is open to plural and contradictory interpretations.

Contrary to Leiter's approach, other scholars have argued that the meaning of *homo natura* is disclosed by reference to Nietzsche's remarks on the natural history of the human species, modelled on his genealogy of morals. Rather than being naturalised as a biological entity that falls under the laws of evolution, here human nature is revealed as radically historical, and the knowledge of the basic text *homo natura* calls for an epistemology capable of capturing the inherent historicity of human nature (Brusotti 2013).

Chapter 1 displaces this debate between naturalist and historicist readings of Nietzsche by adopting Foucault's reconstruction of the emergence of human and biological sciences in the eighteenth and nineteenth centuries. Foucault's claim is that Kant founded the possibility of human sciences by introducing an idea of the human being as an empirical-transcendental doublet that turns human nature itself into the 'truth of truth'.[3] I argue that neither the scientistic nor the historicist interpretations of *homo natura* can avoid Foucault's critique of the Kantian anthropological foundation of the human sciences. Both the scientistic naturalist and the radical historicist readings of Nietzsche's formula separate the question of *homo* (as transcendental) from the question of *natura* (as empirical). In this sense, they fail to capture the break with Kant expressed in Nietzsche's *homo natura*.[4]

This book adopts and defends a third approach to the question of human nature in Nietzsche and its break from the presuppositions of Kantian anthropology. At the centre of this approach is not the theoretical question of whether scientific naturalism or scientific historicism is the most appropriate way of approaching *homo natura*, but the anthropological question concerning the whole nature (*ganze Natur*) of the human being (Riedel 1996; Löwith 1933). Philosophical anthropology takes its starting point from Nietzsche's conception of life and embodiment as situated beyond the Kantian dichotomy between the empirical and the transcendental. It rejects the separation of *homo* from *natura*, practical from theoretical philosophy.[5] From its viewpoint, *homo natura* refers to the impossible separation between the question of the nature of the human being and the question of living a more natural life.

Chapter 1 ties Karl Löwith's insight with respect to Nietzsche's philosophical project to a consideration of Foucault's own trajectory, which led him from his early archaeology of the human sciences to his later biopolitical approach to the Cynics through an interrogation of the practice of *parrhesia*, which Nietzsche translates through his concept of probity or *Redlichkeit*. In the early text on Kant's anthropology, Foucault proposed that Nietzsche puts an end to the anthropological illusion that finds in human nature an essential truth: 'the trajectory of the question *Was ist der Mensch?* in the field of philosophy reaches its end in the response which both challenges and disarms it: *der Übermensch*' (Foucault 2008: 124). This book argues that a crucial step towards understanding the

Nietzschean motif of the overhuman is the idea of *homo natura* and of a more natural humanity. By following the guiding thread of *Redlichkeit*, Chapter 1 suggests that Nietzsche's model for *homo natura* and for a truthful enquiry into the nature of the human being may have been inspired by the ancient Cynics' practice of self-knowledge and truth-telling (*parrhesia*) where the philosophical life exemplifies a natural, lived and embodied pursuit of truth.[6]

Chapter 2, 'Humanism beyond Anthropocentrism', discusses the conception of *homo natura* as a more natural form of human life in relation to Nietzsche's polemic against Christianity, considered as an anti-natural form of civilisation. The argument begins by identifying the terrible element of the 'basic text of *homo natura*' with cruelty, which Nietzsche argues is an essential moment of knowledge and culture. However, Nietzsche's discourse on cruelty is not intended to serve as a criterion to 'select' a higher 'human all too human' type, but instead is employed by Nietzsche to shed a humanist construal of philosophical anthropology. Chapter 2 argues that Löwith's interpretation ignores the role played by animal and even plant life within Nietzsche's idea of the 'more natural' human being as a creator of culture. According to Nietzsche's philosophy of culture, the cultural productivity of the human being derives from the cruelty of the animal as much as from the drive to incorporate, grow and reproduce characteristic of plant life. The retranslation of the human being to nature is thus interpreted in terms of a recovery of animality and even plant life that decentres the privilege of the human species in the continuum of life.

This internal critique to the anthropocentric construal of Nietzsche's philosophical anthropology is registered at the level of literary anthropology. Chapter 2 adopts Wolfgang Riedel's hypothesis that Nietzsche's turn to a philosophy of life, and

I argue also a biopolitics, is not determined by Nietzsche's direct absorption and application of the emerging biological sciences. Instead, it was always mediated by the absorption by literary modernity of the results of the biological sciences, and in this literary form, the philosophy of nature takes on a poetic form that is ultimately expressed in Nietzsche's conception of the Dionysian ground of nature. In other words, *homo natura* is premised on the idea of nature itself becoming artistic.

Chapter 3, 'Psychoanalysis and the Deconstruction of Human Nature', thematises the reception of *homo natura* in Freudian psychoanalysis. Drawing on Ludwig Binswanger's consideration of human nature as *homo natura* in Nietzsche and Sigmund Freud, this chapter argues that Nietzsche's and also Freud's project of the renaturalisation of the human being, and, more generally, of culture, does not reflect a conception of human nature that begins and ends with the natural scientific views of nature. Nietzsche and Freud do employ natural science to deconstruct the civilisational ideal of humanity as superior to animals and plants. However, they both set aside natural science when it comes to reconstructing human nature from out of its place among animals and plants, because natural science is unable to account for human cultural productivity. The central hypothesis here is that the question of human cultural productivity takes both Nietzsche and Freud back to the Greeks and their mythological conception of nature as chaos. Chapter 3 concludes on the figure of the overhuman in Nietzsche as an example of how one could envisage human (self-)transformation that draws on nature as a source for cultural renewal.

Nietzsche envisages the naturalisation of the human being, its retranslation back into nature, as a liberating experience where the human being rediscovers nature as a creative and transformative force that the human being can embody. Nietzsche and Freud ask under what conditions the human being can become human again. For Nietzsche, the question of the future of the human being is contingent on whether the human being is capable of re-embodying nature. Chapter 4, 'Biopolitics, Sexuality and Social Transformation', discusses the hypothesis that, for Nietzsche, this embodiment of the human being is always already sexualised and gendered. More precisely, the rediscovery of nature is inseparable from the embodiment of a new idea of sexuality that is inherently transformative. Kant's *Anthropology* also climaxes, in a sense, in a doctrine of sexual difference.[7] The key principle of Kant's 'characteristic of the sexes' is that 'woman wants to dominate, man to be dominated' (Kant [1798] 2006: 306): 'Since nature also wanted to instil the finer feelings that belong to culture – namely those of sociability and propriety – it made this sex man's ruler through her modesty and eloquence in speech and expression' (ibid.). Whereas in Kant, sexuality is naturalised, in Nietzsche one finds the opposite movement: nature is sexualised. This conception of sexuality is common to both Nietzsche's controversial views on gender and sexuality and Johann Jakob Bachofen's discourse on matriarchy (1861). In both authors, one can discern, at one and the same time, a sexualisation of nature and a socialisation of sexuality. In conversation with feminist readings of Nietzsche, this chapter shows that Nietzsche was among the first to identify a biopolitics of domination, where sexuality and associated forms of essentialism about human nature function as a dispositive of domination, and formulate an affirmative biopolitics, where sexuality is no longer bound by preconceived ideas of gender and where a renewed embodiment of nature opens up the horizons for social imaginaries of liberation and creative transformation.

Throughout the book I argue that for Nietzsche, the human being belongs entirely to nature and is an inseparable part of nature. As in evolutionary theory, by replacing the human being within nature, Nietzsche rejects all teleological narratives and appeals to transcendence that characterises metaphysical and religious approaches to the meaning of human life in order to answer the question, 'what is the human being?'. As in evolutionary theory, for Nietzsche there is no essence to the human being. From the perspective of nature, the very idea of 'the' human being is questionable: 'Human beings do not exist, for there was no first "human being": thus infer the animals' (KSA 10:12[1].95). Yet, whereas in evolutionary theory the becoming of life is determined by the effects of random variations together with their successful or failed adaptation to their environment, Nietzsche argues that human becoming is tied to the relation between its artistic or cultural productivity and notions of nature as chaos and abyss, and is mediated by (human) animality.

The continuum between nature and culture made possible by recognising the animality, and even plant-like being, of the human is linked by Nietzsche with a normative conception of nature. Thus, the question 'what is the human being?' becomes for him the question of 'what is natural to the human being?' or 'who is the natural human being?'. Nietzsche does not seek answers to this question in the past of the human species because he believes that what comes naturally to the human is a capacity for transformation and metamorphosis of its way of being. The naturalisation of the human species thus entails a decentring of its humanity with respect to its life: it signals the advent of posthumanism.

In the Conclusion, 'Posthumanism and Community of Life', I examine contemporary posthumanism as a critical discourse. From my point of view, contemporary posthumanism brings together all the above motifs already found in Nietzsche: a rejection of anthropocentrism, anthropomorphism and species hierarchy based on an idea of a continuum between nature and culture; a rejection of Kantian humanism in favour of a transformative, self-overcoming vision of the human; and, last but not least, a normative intent which seeks to redefine the possibility of an acting subject in contrast to a mere attribute of adaptation to given circumstances, without which posthumanism would cease to be a critical discourse (Braidotti 2016: 13–15; Wolfe 2010).

Yet, despite contemporary posthumanist discourse having a common precursor in Nietzsche's *homo natura*, and somewhat simplifying its many currents, it is possible to say that posthumanism is also divided with respect to how it recovers its Nietzschean legacy of anti-humanism and anti-anthropomorphism. The Conclusion stages one possible representation of this division, which I shall describe in terms of the opposition between a 'biopolitical' posthumanism and, for lack of a better word, an 'assemblage' posthumanism. In contrast to assemblage posthumanism, I argue that a biopolitical posthumanism is of political relevance today not only as a critical discourse that questions civilisational forms of domination, but also as an affirmative discourse that opens up new ways of thinking about a community of life that is shared between humans, animals, plants and other forms of life.

Notes

1　Aphorism 230 of *Beyond Good and Evil: Prelude to a Philosophy of the Future* is reproduced in full in the Appendix of this book.
2　Aphorism 14 of *The Antichrist* is reproduced in full in the Appendix of this book.
3　'But what Kant ambiguously designated as "natural" in that emergence had been forgotten as a fundamental form of the relationship to the object

and resurrected as the "nature" in human nature. As a result, instead of being defined by the movement that criticises it in the context of a reflection on knowledge, the illusion was submitted to an anterior level where it re-emerged as both divided and grounded: it had become the truth of truth – henceforth, truth would be always present and yet never given; thus the illusion has become both the raison d'être and the source of critical thinking, the origin of that movement by which the human being loses sight of and is incessantly recalled to truth' (Foucault 2008: 123).

4 For a different view, see Gori (2015), who argues that Nietzsche's treatment of the question of the human being in *Twilights of the Idols* is in many ways comparable to Kant's idea of a pragmatic anthropology.

5 Helmut Heit makes a similar point when he follows Günter Abel, who argues that Nietzsche's conception of the organic continuum of life reflects 'a naturalisation beyond the dichotomy of transcendental metaphysics and reductionist physicalism' (Abel 2001: 7, as cited in Heit 2014: 36; 27–46). Otherwise, Heit's chapter follows the structure of Kant's four questions of philosophy: 1. What can I know? 2. What shall I do? 3. What may I hope? 4. What is the human being?

6 The question of how to translate the German term *Redlichkeit* into English and how best to grasp its meaning for Nietzsche has been the subject of much discussion in Nietzsche scholarship. Alan White (2001) suggests translating *Redlichkeit* as honesty and ascribes it to the realm of Nietzsche's morality or ethics. Jean-Luc Nancy (1990) also understands *Redlichkeit* as constitutive of Nietzsche's morality but translates it as probity. Neither of the two translations is satisfying insofar as they fail to render the meaning of *Rede* (speech or talk). As a form of speaking the truth before others, *Redlichkeit* in Nietzsche very much resonates with the Greek virtue of *parrhesia*. It is thanks to Michel Foucault's latest analysis of *parrhesia*, that is, frank speech or truth-telling, in classical Greek philosophy, and in particular in the Cynics, that we can appreciate the public and political importance of *Redlichkeit* in Nietzsche (Foucault 2011). This political meaning of *Redlichkeit* has often been overlooked simply due to the fact that *Redlichkeit* has been translated as honesty. Throughout this book, I translate *Redlichkeit* as probity to highlight this public and political dimension of speaking the truth in Nietzsche.

7 See Kant ([1798] 2006: 306–11), in particular the long section dedicated to the 'character of the sexes', where sexual difference – and this means essentially the female sex – is employed by nature to attain two ends: the preservation of the species and 'the cultivation of society and its refinement by womankind' (ibid.: 306).

1

Kantianism, Naturalism and Philosophical Anthropology

When Immanuel Kant revolutionised epistemology by connecting the possibility of knowledge of the objective world to the finitude of the human subject, to our ignorance of the in itself of Nature and of God, he also thereby opened up the question of what it means to know human finitude, that is, he inaugurated the possibility of the human sciences. Michel Foucault began his intellectual trajectory by working on Kant's pragmatic anthropology, and then with *The Order of Things* offered an archaeology of the human sciences. Through his analysis of Kant's anthropology, Foucault identified the main problem with the human sciences. By approaching human activity and behaviour through a positivistic, scientific analysis that generates empirical knowledge of the human being (for example, in the form of economic science), the human being is at the same time transformed into the source of a truth, into a nature, that lies beyond all empirical falsification.

An illustration of this process whereby the scientific knowledge of human finitude naturalises the human being is the idea of *homo oeconomicus*, which models the economic nature of the human being as a natural being. As Gary Becker explains, the extension of the economic approach to all areas of human activity is based on 'assumptions of maximizing behaviour, market equilibrium, and stable preferences' (Becker 1996: 5). If one considers these assumptions purely from an economics standpoint, then there follow well-known theorems of neo-classical economics: a rise in price reduces quantity demanded; a rise in price increases quantity supplied; competitive markets satisfy consumer preferences more effectively than monopoly markets; tax on the output of a market reduces the output, and so on. For Becker, it is not simply that some human behaviour can be profitably analysed along economic lines, but rather, the possibility of economic science requires that the human being be revealed essentially as an economic being, a *homo oeconomicus*, in all areas of activity.

This belief nicely illustrates what Foucault meant when he argued in *The Order of Things* that the human sciences turn the human being into an 'empirico-transcendental doublet'. In his introduction to Kant's *Anthropology*, he writes that as empirical knowledge, the human science 'is the knowledge of man, in a movement which objectifies man on the level of his natural being and in the contents of his animal determinations' (Foucault 2008: 117). However, as transcendental knowledge of finitude, the human science doubles as 'the knowledge of the knowledge of man, and so can interrogate the subject himself, ask him where his limitations lie, and about what he sanctions of the knowledge we have of him' (ibid.). In this second form, Kant's question 'what is the human being?' hides what Foucault calls an 'anthropological illusion' that makes possible the critical enterprise towards the knowledge of the objective world by assuming a transcendental reality of the human being itself: critique has 'locked itself into subjectivity by conceiving of it as thickened, essentialized, enclosed in the impassable structure of

14

menschliches Wesen, in which that extenuated truth which is the truth of truth keeps vigil and gathers itself' (ibid.: 123). By generating this *sui generis* concept of the *homo* (*oeconomicus, politicus, ludens, sexualis*, and so on), the human sciences both separate the human being from other animals as a subject of knowledge in a way that was not the case with the ancients, for whom the human being was still a *zoon* or *animal* that could be qualified in some way or another: as *politikon* or as *sociale et politicum*, and replace it back in nature as an object of empirical study.[1]

This book argues that Friedrich Nietzsche's formula *homo natura* intends to offer an approach to the self-knowledge of human beings that leaves behind the anthropological illusion that, according to Foucault, captivates the human sciences after Kant. The crucial element that distinguishes Nietzsche's *homo natura* from the human nature studied by human sciences is the novel take on the intellectual virtue of probity (*Redlichkeit*). As Leo Strauss defines it, probity is 'this new fortitude, being the willingness to look man's forsakenness in its face, being the courage to welcome the terrible truth, being toughness against the inclination of man to deceive himself about his situation' (Strauss 1995: 37).[2] In aphorism 230 of *Beyond Good and Evil*, Nietzsche argues that in order to translate the human being back to nature, the new scientists will have to display the virtue of probity and pose the question of '"why have knowledge at all?"' (BGE 230). The nature out of which the human being is to understand itself will not be the empirical-transcendental human nature of the kind represented by the idea of *homo oeconomicus*. The knowledge associated by Nietzsche with probity can be contraposed to Kant's anthropological knowledge, which is pragmatic because it is intended to offer the human being a map or orientation in order to fulfil the moral destiny promised by its transcendental character (Cohen 2008).[3] The nature of Nietzsche's *homo natura*, instead, is '*schrecklich*', both terrible and terrifying, for at least two reasons: it accepts no separation between animals and humans, and it grants the human being no special moral destiny. For Nietzsche, it is not possible to separate the question of the human being from the question of knowledge posed by the virtue of probity. Probity understands the possibility of knowledge always already from within the perspective of the human being as a living being.

If *Beyond Good and Evil* 230 suggests that knowing ourselves as creatures of nature requires probity, it is because probity is a 'most spiritual will to power and overcoming of the world (*geistiger Wille zur Macht und Weltüberwindung*)' (BGE 227). Probity produces knowledge that changes the nature of the human being. Only when the will to knowledge becomes self-reflective and takes on the features of nature as will to power, does knowledge release nature's creative potential for the generation and creation of life within the human being and realise the extraordinary force of metamorphosis (*Verwandlung*), of overcoming and self-overcoming. The metamorphosis of human nature is therefore what I take to be the main point of Nietzsche's quest for *homo natura* and of the task of retranslating the human being back into nature. In other words, Nietzsche's answer to the question of 'why knowledge at all?' is the metamorphosis of human nature. Nietzsche confirms in the aphorism following 230 that '[L]earning changes (*verwandelt*) us' (BGE 231).

However, if the turn to *homo natura* is a demand of probity, it is also the case that, conversely, the return to nature orients the human being towards self-knowledge as becoming self-reflective of life itself. The task of translating the human being back into nature thus stands under the Socratic motto: Know thyself!

Nietzsche holds that this knowledge is produced by life and not derived from a transcendental subject. Self-knowledge reflects a drive of life towards growth and generation that alters the nature of the human being.

Once again, it is Foucault's own philosophical trajectory that offers a guiding thread to the interpretation of *Beyond Good and Evil* 230 as a break from Kantianism. For in his last lectures at the Collège de France, entitled *The Government of Self and Others*, Foucault offered a new approach to the ancient Greek 'fundamental principle of *gnothi seauton* (self-knowledge)' by linking it with the history of *parrhesia* or 'free-spokenness' (Foucault 2010: 43), and with the practice of 'care of self': 'One cannot take care of oneself without knowing oneself' (ibid.: 44). Interestingly, Foucault begins his lectures on *parrhesia* by giving an interpretation of Kant's motto of the Enlightenment, 'Dare to know!', which culminates in the division of labour between private obedience, meaning obedience within public institutions, and public freedom of thought, meaning freedom to speak to humanity as such. He then ends his lecture cycle, *The Courage of Truth*, with a discussion of Cynic *parrhesia* as the culmination of this ancient tradition of self-knowledge.

Although in these lectures Foucault never mentions Nietzsche's concept of *Redlichkeit*, this is the term that best translates *parrhesia*. In this chapter, I argue that this curious movement from Kantianism to Cynicism in Foucault makes sense if one understands Nietzsche's discourse on probity and *homo natura* as the decisive locus that offers a different 'way out of the condition of tutelage' that Kant mentions in 'What is Enlightenment?' (Foucault 2011: 26–8). As I discuss at the end of this chapter, *Beyond Good and Evil* 230 suggests that Nietzsche's conception of probity may have been inspired by the ancient Cynics and their vision of the honest and outspoken natural human being. My thesis is that probity, as Nietzsche conceives it, reflects a form of lived and embodied knowledge that keeps us honest and hence open to the continuous task of having to reinvent our nature. In this sense, the Cynic form of life is the best expression for what Nietzsche meant by *homo natura* and offers a form of self-knowledge as the self-reflection of life itself.

Over the last decades, the meaning of *homo natura* has taken centre stage in discussion among Nietzsche scholars. This discussion has largely been dominated by three positions. First, there are accounts of human nature that revolve around the question of Nietzsche's naturalism and its relation to the life sciences and Darwinism in the nineteenth century (Emden 2014; Leiter 2013). Second, Marco Brusotti among others argues that Nietzsche develops his conception of human nature out of an idea of natural history as a 'history of discipline and breeding (*Zucht und Züchtung*)' carried forth by the human species on itself, in an effort to perfect itself (Brusotti 2013, 2014). The perspective on *homo natura* advanced by natural history conceives of human nature as an inherently historical and social construction that requires an epistemology able to capture this historicity and situatedness of human nature (Brusotti 2013, 2014). In what follows I argue that both the (natural-)scientific and the (natural-)historical approaches to *homo natura* fall within a Kantian understanding of anthropology and the problem of providing objective knowledge into the nature of the human being as nature's lawgiver.

In contrast, the third approach to the question of *homo natura* in Nietzsche is advanced by readings, like those of Karl Löwith and Ludwig Binswanger, that situate Nietzsche's philosophy as a form of philosophical anthropology.[4] I defend, here and in the next chapters, the claims that the approach of philosophical anthropology is the closest to what Nietzsche envisaged with his idea of *homo natura*. What stands at the centre of the approach of philosophical anthropology is not the theoretical question of how to know the human being as a natural being, but the anthropological question of the 'whole nature (*ganze Natur*)' of the human being (Riedel 1996). Philosophical anthropology takes its starting point from Nietzsche's conception of the embodied character of all knowledge in order to place its questioning of human nature beyond the Kantian dichotomy between the empirical and the transcendental. Both natural-scientific and natural-historical accounts of Nietzsche's naturalism end up separating the question of *homo* from the question of *natura*, the practical from the theoretical aspects of Nietzsche's philosophy. However, from the standpoint of philosophical anthropology, as I understand it, Nietzsche's *homo natura* reflects a rejection of the separation of *homo* from *natura* and of practical from theoretical philosophy. However, as I show at the end of this chapter, the standpoint of philosophical anthropology itself requires to be complemented with a reading of *homo natura* that highlights Nietzsche's debt to a Greek conception of self-knowledge, and in particular to his appropriation of the ideal of probity and embodied truth found in the ancient Cynics.

Human Nature and Natural Science

Recent debates on human nature in Nietzsche usually start from Brian Leiter's 'negative thesis' on aestheticism, a position he associates with Alexander Nehamas's *Nietzsche: Life as Literature* but that ultimately goes back to 'the influence of writers such as Jacques Derrida, Sarah Kofman, Paul de Man and Richard

Rorty'.[5] According to the standpoint of aestheticism, Nietzsche looks at the world as if it were a literary text and thus arrives at a conception of the human being that reflects generalisations that apply to the literary situation, to the creation and interpretation of literary texts and characters (Leiter 1992: 275–6). While Leiter agrees that as a philologist Nietzsche often speaks metaphorically of the world as a text to be interpreted (ibid.: 276), the issue for him is that Nietzsche is interpreting a 'natural world with particular sorts of natural attributes (for example BGE 230; A 14)' (ibid.: 278). Leiter invokes aphorisms *Beyond Good and Evil* 230 and *The Antichrist* 14 as evidence that Nietzsche's most important philosophical imperative is naturalism.[6] On Leiter's reading, *homo natura* reflects Nietzsche's naturalistic conception of the human being as a 'natural organism'. Leiter suggests that, 'Nietzsche wants to establish a proper starting point for knowledge' (ibid.: 279). In other words, for Leiter Nietzsche's call for probity is to be understood as an extension of the Kantian problem of establishing the knowledge of man on a proper scientific, that is, naturalistic footing, rather than calling into question the human will to knowledge from the perspective of nature and of life.

Leiter's negative thesis on aestheticism is complemented by his positive thesis on naturalism, according to which human behaviour and values are causally determined by 'heritable psychological and physiological traits' or what he also refers to as 'type-facts' (Knobe and Leiter 2007: 89–90). On this view, Nietzsche's naturalistic project is concerned with explaining how and why a certain type of person comes to bear certain values and ideas just as 'one might come to understand things about a certain type of tree by knowing its fruits' (Leiter 2002: 10). Leiter thus concludes that 'just as natural facts about the tree explain the fruit it bears, so too type-facts about a person will explain the ideas and values he comes to bear' (ibid.).

Leiter's interpretation of *homo natura* seems to fall neatly within Foucault's analysis of the Kantian bases of human sciences. Foucault argued that Kant, in order to criticise the transcendental illusion which places the source of truth and meaning outside of human knowledge, ended up generating an anthropological illusion by turning human nature itself into the truth of truth: 'all knowledge of man is presented [. . .] as always invested with a meaning which has to do with the return to the origin, to the authentic, to the founding activity, to the reason why there is meaning in the world' (Foucault 2008: 123–4). The human sciences, in this sense, would be constitutive of this anthropological illusion. According to Foucault, such theories, including scientific naturalism, reflect a naturalistic reduction of 'man's transcendental side to its empirical aspect': 'this true discourse finds its foundation and model in the empirical truth whose genesis in nature and in history it retraces, so that one has an analysis of the positivist type' (Foucault 1994b: 320). As Beatrice Han-Pile has pointed out, Foucault criticises such an attempt for its essentialism, and for unduly turning 'man' into a mere object of nature (Han-Pile 2010: 130). It is important to note that Foucault does not direct his critique against anthropology per se but against the anthropologism at the heart of Kantian and neo-Kantian constructions of the human being as a transcendental subject. On Foucault's hypothesis, the understanding of the human being as a transcendental subject of knowledge provides the foundation for subsequent positivistic accounts of the human being as a mere object of nature.

From the perspective of Foucault's critical remarks, Leiter's naturalistic conception of *homo natura* understood as a living organism whose natural attributes are accessible through the empirical sciences provides an example of such a positivistic anthropology. The naturalistic understanding of the human being along the continuum of the natural world leads to a reversal of the dependence-relation between art and nature. Leiter holds that 'nature is not to be construed artistically; rather the work of art is to be understood naturalistically (as a product of the "basic instincts of power, nature")' (Leiter 1992: 284). This reversal, however, indicates the extent to which Leiter's naturalism remains within the scope of Foucault's critique: by positing the nature of the human being as the starting point of knowledge, Leiter's naturalism ends up turning the human being into a mere object of nature.

Scientistic or reductionist naturalism discounts the self-reflective dimension of knowledge in the living human being and thus arrives at a deterministic account of Nietzsche's conception of human nature unable to provide an explanation of the metamorphosis of the human being. This may explain why for Leiter there are 'Two Nietzsches' – a theoretical and a practical one, a naturalistic and an anti-naturalistic Nietzsche (Leiter 2013: 582–4). Leiter holds that Nietzsche's speculative psychology – for example, what Nietzsche thinks explains the genesis of our current morality, how Nietzsche understands the mechanisms of human psychology, what he takes to be the causal consequences of moral beliefs, and so on – is not the ultimate goal of his philosophical project. Rather, it is subordinated to and complementary with what Leiter refers to as Nietzsche's therapeutic project – for example, to produce a therapeutic effect on his readers and to free them from their false consciousness about the dominant morality (ibid.: 582). Leiter argues that the fact that both projects are often mixed up in Nietzsche's texts does not provide a good reason to contest separating them out in principle as two distinct branches of Nietzsche's philosophy. He offers the example of Sigmund Freud's psychoanalytical enquiries to illustrate this point. Whereas Freud and Nietzsche share much of the same ground in that they both operate on the basis of a naturalist psychology, the difference between the two is that the practice of psychoanalysis is the place of therapy in Freud, in contrast to Nietzsche, who relies on his books to produce a double effect: to enlighten by means of his methodological and sceptical naturalism and to heal by means of his philosophical rhetoric and style. I discuss the question of the relation between Nietzsche and Freud and the question of whether their psychology is indeed naturalistic in Chapter 3, where I distinguish between the deconstructive and reconstructive dimensions of Nietzsche's and Freud's naturalisms in psychology. The point I wish to make here is that Leiter's naturalism and his understanding of Nietzsche's theoretical conception of human nature is entirely oriented towards the past, towards providing knowledge of what we are as creatures of nature. As such, it fails to capture the future-oriented dimension of Nietzsche's thinking about human nature that seeks to renaturalise the human being in view of recreating 'a natural and genuine humanity' (BT X).

Furthermore, Leiter's reading of Nietzsche's therapeutic motif is also backward insofar as it may dispel illusions of morality that Nietzsche seeks to overcome through a transformative conception of naturalism 'beyond good and evil'. Leiter's critique of normativity is unable to articulate a new normativity, 'a natural and genuine humanity', that would allow us to overcome the discontents of our civilisation.

Human Nature and Natural History

On the question of human nature in Nietzsche, the position of Brusotti provides a reconstruction of the meaning of *homo natura* in the context of Nietzsche's attempt to provide a natural history of morals. Brusotti offers a reading of Nietzsche's naturalism that is critical of Leiter's reductionist type-facts approach to the discourse of moral types in Nietzsche, and at the same time seeks to maintain a closer relation between Nietzsche's naturalism and his normativism based on the virtue of probity that characterises the free spirits than is found in Leiter's 'two Nietzsches' claims (Brusotti 2011, 2013, 2014). Brusotti puts forward a convincing case for a different consideration of Nietzsche's overall philosophical methodology that is based both on a critique of the natural sciences and on an attempt to profoundly rethink the relationship between the natural and the human sciences in the form of natural history.[7]

For Brusotti, Nietzsche's attempt to 'renaturalize' the human being sits within a more general project of determining 'the natural history of morals', and, even more particularly, to determine the 'natural history of the free spirit' (Brusotti 2014: sect. 7.2; Brusotti 2013: sect. 5). By natural history, Brusotti means, in the first instance, the collection and surveying of a great variety of moralities in Nietzsche so as to be able to investigate what lies beneath the phenomenon of moral behaviour. This is the historical aspect of natural history. The natural aspect of a natural history of morals is the discovery of effective historical forces behind this variety of moralities, which essentially amount to the two types of master and slave moralities. Here Brusotti claims that Nietzsche's 'tendency to typology' is quite close to his contemporaneous 'evolutionary anthropology' with its 'universal scale of cultural progress (*universellen Stufenleiter kulturellen Fortschritts*)' (Brusotti 2014: sect. 7.2). Lastly, this binary typology leads Nietzsche to a normative articulation of *homo natura* as the 'repressed basic type (*verdrängten Grundtypus*)' of the master morality that needs to be brought back to light according to Brusotti. This typological approach to natural history culminates in the key distinction of a 'natural history of morality', namely Nietzsche's discourse on the 'degeneration (*Entartung*)' of the 'last man' and the need to 'discipline and breed' an 'overman' understood as the 'higher type' of human being (Brusotti 2014: sect. 7.4). In short, for Brusotti, Nietzsche's *homo natura* is meant to clear the slate from 'mistaken metaphysical anthropologies' (ibid.: sect. 7.5) in order to 'breed' a new higher type of human being identified with the figure of the free spirit.

According to Brusotti, Nietzsche considers the human and the natural sciences as a continuum (Brusotti 2011). Brusotti questions the separation Leiter proposes between Nietzsche's theoretical and practical philosophy, with the former being constitutive of a Humean naturalism that is oriented towards the past, that is, explaining morality naturalistically, and the latter being constitutive of a therapeutic Nietzsche who is preoccupied with the future, that is, the liberation of the human being from the shackles of morality. In contraposition to variants of scientific naturalism, Brusotti argues that the translation of the human being back into nature requires a historical philosophical approach, which encompasses both the naturalisation of the human sciences and the historisation of the natural sciences and thus overcomes the methodological dualism found in Leiter.

Another reason why Brusotti rejects the division of Nietzsche's philosophy into a theoretical and a practical branch is that in

Nietzsche knowledge is self-reflective. The knowledge of *homo natura* discovered by Nietzsche's free spirits is inscribed within their own coming to know themselves, their self-knowledge and their probity towards themselves as creatures of nature. This is also the view of Paul van Tongeren, who argues that aphorism *Beyond Good and Evil* 230 features a 'naturalisation of probity' (van Tongeren 2014: 162).

In *Beyond Good and Evil* 230, Nietzsche describes the tragic dilemma of the seekers of knowledge (*Erkennende*) who, confronted with the 'terrible basic text of human nature', need to come to terms with the fact that their so-called probity is just a 'beautiful, glittering, jingling, festive' word beneath which the seeker of knowledge discovers that 'there is something cruel in the inclination of my spirit' (BGE 230).[8] Before the task of translating the human being back into nature, the free spirits face a paradox. On the one hand, probity is required in order to see the nature of the human being as *homo natura*. But, on the other hand, to complete the translation of the human being back into nature also requires the overcoming of the belief in probity as an artefact of human culture. As such, the naturalisation of probity implies both the highest realisation of probity and the self-overcoming of probity towards an unknown and uncertain future beyond good and evil. For both van Tongeren and Brusotti, the translation of the human being back into nature calls for a (self-)overcoming of probity understood as a moral virtue. Nietzsche's free spirits are not only tasked with increasing the knowledge of past moralities, as Leiter's naturalistic reading claims, but also with the embodiment of a morality of the future, namely, 'a postmoral morality, embodied by the free, very free sprits Nietzsche longs for' (Brusotti 2014: 130).

Brusotti's reading of *homo natura* acknowledges the open question of how a return to nature may produce a postmoral morality. However, his reading remains focused on the past, the natural history of human morals. Furthermore, Brusotti's reading of *homo natura* shares with Leiter's reading a similar shift from the question of human nature to the question of knowledge. He replaces 'the more general problem – the human being as *homo natura*' (Brusotti 2013: 270) with the more specific question of the natural history of the subject of knowledge (*Erkennende*). This may explain why for Brusotti the answer to the question of 'why knowledge at all?' can be found in Nietzsche's discussion of the natural history of knowledge found in the preceding aphorism, *Beyond Good and Evil* 229. Brusotti adds that in a previous draft of aphorisms 229 and 230, their order was reversed: 'There exists in Nietzsche's view no "better answer" to this natural historical question as the reference to the fact that the *seeker of knowledge* turns his own cruelty against himself, against the basic will of the spirit' (ibid.: 277, my emphasis).

As such, Brusotti's reading of aphorism 230 produces a problem similar to the one found in Leiter's scientistic naturalism. By treating the question of knowledge as separate from the more general question of the human being, Brusotti provides a one-sided interpretation of aphorism 230. Both Leiter's scientistic naturalism and Brusotti's natural history are primarily concerned with the question of knowledge as separate from the question of human nature. Whereas Leiter's focus is on *natura* and thus ends up reducing the human being to a mere object of nature, Brusotti's focus is on *homo* (the seeker of knowledge) and thus may run the risk of reducing the human being to a (transcendental) subject of knowledge.

Human Nature and Philosophical Anthropology

From the perspective of philosophical anthropology, the question of human nature cannot be separated from the question of human knowledge, just like practical philosophy cannot be separated from theoretical philosophy. This is because philosophical anthropology considers the human being as a living being that produces knowledge which is lived and reflected in nature. In an article on Søren Kierkegaard and Nietzsche published in 1933, Löwith provides a reading of *Beyond Good and Evil* 230 that identifies Nietzsche's conception of the human being as *homo natura* with the emergence of philosophical anthropology. Löwith argues that the intimate connection between knowledge and life characteristic of Kierkegaard's and Nietzsche's thinking is reflected in their conceptions of life and existence, the two 'basic concepts (*Grundbegriffe*)' of their philosophies (Löwith 1933). Kierkegaard and Nietzsche understand philosophy no longer as a closed metaphysical system that contains, among other sciences, an anthropology. Instead, for Löwith, in Kierkegaard and Nietzsche all the questions of philosophy are gathered up in the one 'basic question (*Grundfrage*)' of what the human being is.

As discussed by Löwith, Nietzsche rejects the figure of the philosopher as metaphysician (exemplified among others by Hegel) who abstracts his life from his philosophical considerations. Against the metaphysical thinker, Löwith upholds the necessity of self-knowledge advanced in Nietzsche's *Dawn*: 'Know thyself is the whole science. Only once the human being has gained knowledge of all things will the human being know itself. For things are nothing but the limits of the human being' (D 48). From this standpoint, knowledge, including the knowledge produced by the natural and human sciences, must be conceived within the human being's experience of itself as a living being. For philosophy this means that truth is produced by and inseparable from the living philosopher's self-experimentations. As such, Nietzsche's overall philosophical project aims at the overcoming of philosophy as a systematic philosophical account of the world that can be separated from the perspective of its author: philosophy becomes an experimental psychology (ibid.: 43).

According to Löwith, a consequence of the radical 'humanisation (*Vermenschlichung*) of philosophy' in Kierkegaard and Nietzsche is that the problem of truth is reduced to the problem of probity, with probity being the only remainder in the former belief in truth (ibid.: 43–4).[9] At stake in *Beyond Good and Evil* is a transformation of a pure philosophy of spirit into a multifaceted philosophy of the human being whose authors understand themselves as both 'last' and 'future' philosophers. Truth as probity withdraws the ground of philosophy as the pursuit of truth. However, Löwith quickly adds that this tragic loss of truth also announces a new beginning for philosophy understood as philosophical anthropology (ibid.: 46).[10] In *Beyond Good and Evil* 230, this new beginning depends on whether the free spirits Nietzsche longs for will be able to enact a return to nature that overcomes the Christian worldview and its morality towards the becoming of a more natural humanity.

Löwith seems to agree with Nietzsche's philosophical approach to the question of human nature. However, he laments that Nietzsche's *homo natura* does not provide a coherent account of the naturalness of the human being and concludes that Nietzsche's conception of human nature remains polemical, reactive and ultimately caught up within its opposition to the Christian moral worldview. In particular, Nietzsche's conception of life is, according to Löwith, 'vague' and 'indeterminate', oscillating between purely naturalistic and physiological explanations of the human and an articulation of a moralistic/immoralistic interpretation of the world. As if anticipating the tenor and assumptions of the much later debate within Nietzschean scholarship on *homo natura* that I delineated above, Löwith claims that in comparison with Kierkegaard, Nietzsche is like a 'dilettante positivistic Neo-Kantian' who did not go far enough in the overcoming of neo-Kantianism (ibid.: 64).

The shortcomings of Löwith's reading of Nietzsche's *homo natura* as a philosophical anthropology are discussed in Chapter 2. Here, I am simply concerned with making the point that Löwith's initial reading of *homo natura* and the problem of self-knowledge does not sufficiently take into account the Greek influence on Nietzsche's thinking about truth, nature and the philosophical life. For Nietzsche, nature is no longer simply an object of scientific enquiry but a force that transpires all aspects of human existence. He seeks to capture this excess of nature through the philosophical concept of life.[11] *Beyond Good and Evil* 230 articulates a conception of the philosophical life — exemplified by the figure of the free spirit — where probity advances the paradoxical and open task of the continuous invention and reinvention of the human being through a return to nature. In my view, Nietzsche's vision of the philosophical life and of *homo natura* may find a precursor in the Cynic Diogenes of Sinope, the prototype of the philosopher as a *homo natura*. Commentators have typically pointed out the affinities between Nietzsche's and the Cynics' philosophical styles as well as their projects of transvaluation. I wish to complement these readings by offering a comparison of their anthropologies.[12]

Human Nature and Probity

The ancient Cynics provide an example of the philosophical life and of probity as lived and embodied truth where the return to nature is oriented towards the future and enables a transvaluation of all values including a transvaluation of human nature. For the Cynics, philosophy as the pursuit of truth or knowledge is not a doctrine or science but a form of life and practice. For the Cynics, the question of truth is inseparable from the question of the true life.[13] The question of how truth can be lived is taken literally by the Cynics: they ask how truth can be embodied, and how it can be materialised in the physical body. The naturalisation of truth in the Cynics no doubt resonates, on the one hand, with Nietzsche's view that the life and thought of a philosopher are inseparable, where the pursuit of knowledge can no longer be considered apart from the life of the philosopher, as Löwith points out; and, on the other hand, with Nietzsche's reformulation of the question of truth as the question of whether truth can be embodied (GS 110). For the question of *homo natura* in Nietzsche, this means, first, that there can be no separation between theory and practice in his philosophy and, second, that the question of human nature needs to be investigated from the standpoint of embodiment, of the human being as a living being, a position advanced by philosophical anthropology.

The retranslation of the human being back into nature embodied by Nietzsche's free spirits is comparable to the Cynic philosophers' embodiment of truth which also rests on a return to nature. Interestingly, in the Cynics, this return to nature passes through an overcoming of conventional and hence false interpretations of human nature and is an essential aspect of their understanding of *parrhesia*, the practice of probity or truth-telling.

31

The purpose of the practice of probity in the Cynics is to alter the value of the currency, or, in other words, to overthrow conventional understandings of human nature.[14] The Cynics seek to overcome the barriers that civilisation has erected between nature and the human being. Again, this idea clearly resonates with Nietzsche's vision of the free spirits who are charged with the task to 'become master over the many vain and overly enthusiastic interpretations and connotations that have so far been scrawled and painted over that eternal basic text *homo natura*' (BGE 230). As in the Cynics, in Nietzsche, probity is required to alter established conceptions of human nature. For the question of human nature in Nietzsche, this means that Nietzsche's anthropology is always also an anti-anthropology insofar as it questions established conventions and opinions of what human nature is (Stegmaier and Bertino 2015). It overcomes positivistic and essentialist anthropologies towards a conception of human nature as historical and in becoming.[15] Accordingly, Nietzsche maintains that there can be no final overcoming of error. The question of how far truth can be embodied must remain an open question, an open experiment through which one simultaneously discovers and creates new forms of life (GS 110).

In the Cynics, the self-fashioning of human nature is reflected in the idea that the philosophical life as the true life has the power to change the nature of the human being. For them, an honest pursuit of truth means facing the challenges of self-knowledge as continuous self-experimentation. The Cynics' relentless commitment to self-experimentation led Foucault to the conclusion that for the Cynics the true life is an altered and altering life. But Foucault asks, 'for life to truly be the life of truth, must it not be an *other* life, a life which is radically and paradoxically other?' (Foucault 2011: 245). From my point of view, this idea of alteration is what is at stake in Nietzsche's vision of a metamorphosis of human nature produced through the embodiment of *homo natura* enacted by Nietzsche's free spirits. The return to nature reveals that human nature is multiple, plural and in becoming continuously immersed in alteration and self-alteration and hence never self-same and identical to itself. Through the retranslation of the human being back into nature, Nietzsche's free sprits discover that human nature does not lie behind us as something that pertains to some remote form of (animal or plant) life, but something that lies ahead of us in the future.[16] The question of *homo natura* is not a question of what we are (scientistic naturalism) or how we have become what we are (natural history), but of what else we could become (philosophical anthropology). When Nietzsche calls for the retranslation of the human being back into nature, this backward movement needs to be understood as a movement that is like the tending of a bow: a drawing backward that is oriented towards the future (BGE Preface).

For the Cynics, nature as opposed to convention is the only acceptable standard against which to measure a true life. This standard takes the form of the life of the animal, and, in particular, the life of the dog.[17] The Cynics' invitation to rethink the value of animality, including human animality, reminds us of Nietzsche's invitation to rethink the value of cruelty in aphorism 229 of *Beyond Good and Evil*. In Chapter 2 I will discuss how, in contraposition to western metaphysics, Nietzsche transvalues rather than excludes what the human being has received from nature. Instead of excluding cruelty, Nietzsche advances the thesis that the cruelty of the animal motivates cultural productivity and lies at the basis of all our civilisational achievements. This is the terrible insight that Nietzsche's free spirits admit to when they confirm that even their own quest for knowledge is motivated by cruelty (BGE 229).

Interestingly, all of the abovementioned aspects of Nietzsche's conception of human nature – the inseparability of life and thought, the condition of embodiment, the anti-foundationalist aspect of the return to nature, the transvaluation of values, the becoming of life and the multifaceted character of human nature as well as the continued metamorphosis of the human being – are reflected in Nietzsche's conception of probity. Insofar as these aspects also pertain to the ancient Cynic understanding of probity, I argue that Nietzsche's notion of probity and of the natural human being may have been inspired by the ancient Cynics.

Probity in Nietzsche stands for a commitment to self-experimentation which reflects the inseparability of life and thought in the seeker of knowledge devoted to the study and interpretation of experience:

> As interpreters of our experiences (*Erlebnisse*). One type of probity (*Redlichkeit*) has been alien to all religion-founders and such: they have not made their experiences (*Erlebnisse*) a matter of conscience for their knowledge. [. . .] But we, we others, we reason-thirsty ones, want to face our experiences (*Erlebnisse*) as sternly as we would a scientific experiment (*wissenschaftlichen Versuche*), hour by hour, day by day! We want to be our own experiments and guinea-pigs (*Experimente und Versuchs-Thiere*). (GS 319)[18]

The reference to experience as the starting point for the honest pursuit of truth should not be misunderstood as a falling back into some kind of realism.[19] For Nietzsche, experiences do not reflect a given or underlying truth. On the contrary, facing our experiences as a scientific experiment means acknowledging that all our experiences are based on interested value judgements which are not absolute but always historically situated, constructed and hence false (GS 114).

As in the Cynics, for Nietzsche probity is an embodied truth. Probity is not something exterior to the body, some kind of 'verbal pomp and mendacious pomp' (BGE 230). Instead, probity affirms the naturalness of the human being. For Nietzsche, affirming *homo natura* means embracing the condition of embodiment as pertaining to life rather than hiding the body behind illusions of a higher, moral origin. As in the Cynics, probity implies that individuals 'unlearn shame (*Scham verlernen*)' and refrain from 'denying the naturalness of one's instincts (*natürliche Instinkte verleugnen*)' (KSA 12:10[45]). Nietzsche's motto of probity, 'Let's be naturalistic (*Seien wir naturalistisch*) and let's not paint our inclinations and disinclinations (*Neigungen und Abneigungen*) in moral colors (*moralischen Farbtöpfen*)' (KSA 12:1[90]), qualifies as deliberately Cynic.[20]

Probity as the return to nature stands in tension with established conventions and obligations to commit to institutionalised moral, political, religious or patriarchal values (KSA 9:6[223]). Probity calls for an overcoming of morality (BGE 32), it advances a truth 'beyond good and evil' (Z IV 'Retired'; see also GS 107 as well as KSA 12:2[191]). In contraposition to moral, religious and metaphysical dogmatism, probity is anti-foundationalist: it means thinking against oneself, continuously undermining and questioning one's so-called truth. For Nietzsche, this type of self-critical thinking is a sign of greatness. He exclaims: 'I am not willing to acknowledge any kind of greatness which is not linked to *probity against itself*' (KSA 9:7[53]).

Furthermore, in Nietzsche probity as an embodied truth is conceived as a drive (KSA 9:6[127]) that cannot be abstracted from life and the body (KSA 9:6[130]). Probity means embracing the body as a plurality of drives irreducible to each other and involved in a continuous struggle for and against each other (KSA 9:6[234]). This may be why Nietzsche understands probity as 'something in the process of becoming' (D 456). Probity is transformative and subject to change. But the transformative power of probity does not only concern the life of the individual but also the world and its values. Let's recall that probity is the most spiritual will to power and the will to overcome the world: as such, it is indispensable for the transvaluation of all values (BGE 227). As mentioned above, the theme of transvaluation is one of the key features of Cynic probity reflected in the Cynic philosophers' power to change the 'value of the currency money'. Nietzsche also associates probity with the transvaluation of values.[21]

Nietzsche believes that probity has the power to transform human nature (D 167). But this requires giving up the idea of human nature as something fixed and absolute, something that is defined by a unified essence. Nietzsche thinks of human nature as multiple rather than as unified: 'we cannot feel ourselves anymore as one thing (*Einzigkeit*) of the ego: we are always already among a multiplicity (*Mehrheit*)' (KSA 9:6[80]). For Nietzsche, the return to nature is thus oriented towards the diversification and multiplication of life. Embracing the human being's naturalness and belonging to nature open the possibility for the continuous invention and reinvention of human nature. According to the Cynics, only those who embody the entire cosmos successfully enact a return to nature.[22] Such people live according to the laws of nature and confront conventional and false conceptions of human nature in an open and honest manner. In a note from the 1880s, Nietzsche describes the philosopher who is honest in dealing with himself and with others in similar terms, that is, as someone who embodies the entire cosmos: 'we are the cosmos insofar as we have grasped (*begriffen*) and dreamt it' (KSA 9:6[80]). The character of probity in the philosopher is peculiar. In both the Cynics and Nietzsche, probity manifests itself as an exteriorisation and naturalisation of the philosopher, which is internalised as a pluralising diversification of human nature. The Cynics believe that the return to nature leads to a transformation of the human being, liberating its power to continuously create and recreate its own conditions of existence beyond the struggle of self-preservation towards a freer and more truthful form of life. The intimate connection between nature and liberation that the Cynics intuited may have inspired Nietzsche's vision of the philosopher as a *homo natura*.

Notes

1　For Giorgio Agamben (2004), this double movement of cutting the human from the animal in order to replace the human back in nature as an object of scientific study is the result of what he terms an 'anthropological machine'.

2　Here, Strauss does not cite Nietzsche explicitly on probity, but the expression of 'the terrible truth' seems to be a reference to aphorism 230's 'terrible basic text *homo natura*'.

3　'Following the pragmatic turn operated by Kant's anthropology, the question "what is man?" should be replaced by the question "what can he make of himself?": an enquiry into meaning thus being substituted for an enquiry about essence. This shift entails that the meaning attached to human nature, far from being an immediate given, is now defined as the result from the constructive work that man does freely, "as a citizen of the world", through his actions, his culture and civilisation, on his natural dispositions' (Cohen 2008: 514). However, Alix A. Cohen cites Kant's text in which he clearly states the moral imperative underlying anthropology: 'man is destined by his reason to live in a society of other people, and in this society he has to cultivate himself, civilize himself, and apply himself to a moral purpose by the arts and sciences' (Kant [1798] 2006: 241–2; AA 7:324, cited in Cohen 2008: 514).

4   Here I use the term 'philosophical anthropology' in a broad sense, as used, for example, in Binswanger (1947) and Löwith (1933). For an overview of the different meanings and uses of the term 'philosophical anthropology', see Honenberger (2016). For a comprehensive discussion of Nietzsche's relation to the tradition of philosophical anthropology associated with Max Scheler, Arnold Gehlen and Helmut Plessner, see Schlossberger (1998). On Nietzsche and philosophical anthropology, see also the articles by Fischer (2018) and Krüger (2018).

5   Leiter (1992: 290). While I agree with Leiter's main arguments against Nehamas's aestheticism, the question of whether the positions of Jacques Derrida, Sarah Kofman, Paul de Man and Richard Rorty also fall under Nehamas's aestheticism would require further evidence. On this point see also Helmut Heit (2016: 56–80), who argues that Leiter makes no further approach to reconstruct such receptions, 'but rather implies one must choose between a naturalist or a postmodern Nietzsche' (Heit 2016: 61).

6   On Nietzsche's naturalism, see also Christoph Cox (1999), who also associates BGE 230 with Nietzsche's naturalism, and the call for a 'return to nature' and naturalness as one strand of Nietzsche's philosophical project in contrast to the primacy and irreducibility of interpretation associated with Nietzsche's perspectivism, anti-foundationalism and genealogical method. Cox's thesis is that Nietzsche successfully navigates between relativism and dogmatism, freedom and necessity (Cox 1999: 2, 3, 11): whereas Nietzsche's relativism is 'held in check by his naturalism', his naturalism in turn is 'mitigated by his perspectivism' (ibid.: 3). Although Cox is careful to distinguish Nietzsche's naturalism from scientistic or reductionist accounts, from the perspective of philosophical anthropology, Cox's account is still too dualistic and modelled on a Kantian epistemology.

7   On Nietzsche's conception of historical philosophy and the question of the naturalisation of the human sciences (*Geisteswissenschaften*), see Brusotti (2011) and Christian J. Emden (2014), in particular Emden's discussion of Leiter's

methodological and substantive variant of naturalism in Nietzsche (Emden 2014: 62–6). Emden carefully distinguishes his account of Nietzsche's naturalism from Leiter's reductionist perspective, arguing that Nietzsche's naturalism must be understood within two main contexts: contemporary pluralistic and experimental life sciences, and the critical epistemology of the early Neo-Kantians (Emden 2014: 20, 29). On the shortcomings of Emden's account of Nietzsche's naturalism, see Heit (2016: 56–80).

8   Paul van Tongeren (2014) argues that the term 'terrible (*schrecklich*)' in 'terrible basic text of *homo natura*' is a reference to tragedy and hence points to a tragic rather than a naturalistic conception of nature in BGE 230: 'Certainly, for Nietzsche nature is related to the tragic, and he seeks to return to the experience of the tragic by liberating nature from moral connotations painted over the basic text of *homo natura*' (van Tongeren 2014: 162).

9   On probity in Nietzsche, see also Strauss (1983: chapter 8); Nancy (1990); White (2001); Benoit (2012); Lemm (2018).

10 See also, on the end of man as a new beginning in Nietzsche, Jaspers (1981); Schacht (1995, 2006).

11 On the becoming of life in Nietzsche, see Lemm (2014b, 2015).

12 For an extensive comparison between Nietzsche and the Cynics, see Niehus-Pröbsting (1988: 306–40) and Desmond (2008: 225–34).

13 On the inseparability of theory and practice in the Cynics, see Navia (2005).

14 On the importance of *parrhesia* for Cynicism, see also Branham (1996).

15 Andreas Urs Sommer (2016: 650–.) also rejects the view that BGE 230 provides a textual basis for an essentialist and absolutist anthropology in Nietzsche.

16 Alan White (2001) contests the view that *Redlichkeit* in Nietzsche is associated to truth-telling because truth-telling is an ancient virtue that chronologically goes back to the Persians. White argues that it was the 'Persian virtue' of the historical Zarathustra according to Nietzsche (EH IV 3) and the virtue of the noble Greeks who referred to themselves as 'we truthful ones' (BGE 260, GM I 5), in contrast to *Redlichkeit*, which Nietzsche qualifies as the 'youngest virtue' (Z I 3) (White 2001: 65). But one could argue that the idea of truth-telling as lived and embodied probity is new insofar as Nietzsche claims that we are only now starting to understand that the question of truth means addressing the problem of how truth can be lived and embodied (GS 110). The major innovation of Cynic philosophy is in my view to have inaugurated a new practice of philosophy understood as the challenge to live and embody truth (Lemm 2014a). This

challenge requires the courage not only to see the truth, as Blaise Benoit argues (2012), but also to live and embody it. In the Cynics, the visibility of embodied truth passes through the practice of truth-telling in the public place. As such, *parrhesia* rests on the courage of the Cynic philosopher to speak the truth even if this means that he or she may be exiled from the *polis*. But here White's reading of *Redlichkeit* as the youngest virtue may be reconciled with my reading of *Redlichkeit* in Nietzsche that finds its precursor in Cynic *parrhesia* to the extent that he argues, although not explicitly, that Nietzsche's conception of *Redlichkeit* has important consequences for his understanding of human nature. What *Redlichkeit* teaches us, White remarks, is that 'we are neither rational animals nor logical/linguistic ones; instead, perhaps we are animals that are *redlich*, animals whose telos or perfection is *Redlichkeit*. But whereas we as logical/linguistic animals might aspire to conclusive truth about what is just and right for all human beings in all situations, and we as rational animals might aspire to the mathematical physics that would allow us to become master and possessors of nature, we as *redliche* animals, in Nietzsche's sense, must – if we are to exhibit the *Redlichkeit* that follows from what we are as *redlich* – forsake for such final conclusions and ultimate solutions' (White 2001: 75). For White this means that as '*redliche*' animals we must remain 'cognizant of the perpetual possibility of seeing differently and of naming differently' (ibid.). But this is precisely what the Cynics tried to prove through their physical bodies, through the literal embodiment of truth, namely, to borrow again the phrase from Foucault, that the true life is always another altering and altered life. It is a life cognisant of the perpetual possibility of metamorphosing human nature, a life that resists or, as White puts it, that 'requires insisting on the absence of utterly reliable stabilities or identities' (ibid.: 76).

17   As such, the Cynics' affirmation of a life according to nature is very different to the Stoics' demand to live according to nature that Nietzsche criticises in BGE 9. On the reversal of the hierarchy between gods, humans and animals in the Cynics, see Goulet-Cazé (1996: 61–4).

18   On the lack of probity in religious founders, see also Nietzsche (KSA 9:6[229]).

19   'Probity in art – has nothing to do with realism! Essentially probity of the artist against their powers (*Kräfte*): they do not want to lie to themselves, nor intoxicate themselves – no effect! on themselves, but they want to *imitate* (*nachahmen*) the experience (*Erlebniss*) (the real effect)' (KSA 9:6[244]).

20   Following the example of the Cynics, Nietzsche contests the feeling of
     shame as a means to discipline and tame the naturalness of the human
     being. On this aspect of Cynicism and Nietzsche, see also Sloterdijk
     (1983).

21   On the overcoming of a moral idea of *Redlichkeit* towards a new concep-
     tion of justice in Nietzsche, see Blaise Benoit (2012: 100–3). Although
     Benoit acknowledges that the heroism Nietzsche associates with *Redlich-
     keit* as the courage to face the terrible basic text of nature may remind
     us of the probity of the Cynics, he argues that *Redlichkeit* in Nietzsche
     is derived from virtue in the Renaissance and, in particular, reflects the
     lucidity of Machiavelli's idea of virtue where knowledge is indissociably
     linked up with action, that is, practice. However, one could argue that
     the inseparability of theory and practice is precisely what is at stake in the
     Cynics' reversal of the Platonic conception of philosophy as a discourse on
     the truth of the soul that needs to be abstracted from the life of the body.
     From this point of view, the idea of virtue in the Renaissance would find
     its precursor in the Cynics' practice of philosophy; on this point, see also
     Foucault (2011). As in the Cynics, Nietzsche advocates for a return to
     nature as a path towards self-knowledge that leads to a reconceptualisation
     of human nature and that is inseparable from an inauguration of post- or
     extra-moral forms of life in community with others. But the main goal of
     Benoit's essay is to show that *Redlichkeit* in Nietzsche supremely reflects
     the virtue of the philologist for whom reading a text means 'doing it
     justice *(lire justement)*', which requires both the art of deciphering and of
     fashioning the meaning of the text (Benoit 2012: 107). Benoit points out
     correctly that the figure of the philologist in Nietzsche has a strong affinity
     with the figure of the legislator of the future: in both figures, the art of
     reading well stands for the art of fashioning meaning, of sculpting meaning
     with the help of the hammer (Benoit 2012: 106). From the perspective
     of the philologist, doing justice to the basic text *homo natura* would hence
     require not only deciphering but also fashioning, that is, transforming
     its meaning.

22   For an affirmative reading of Cynic cosmopolitanism, see Moles (1996).

2

Humanism beyond Anthropocentrism

I have argued that recent discussions of Friedrich Nietzsche's naturalism tend to fall prey to a Kantian scheme according to which the knowledge of the *natura* or nature of the human being has to be scientifically secured, either in terms of evolutionary, biological type-facts or in terms of the historical development of moral types, in order to orient the *homo* towards its proper therapy that shall lead the human being to its over-human yet still moral destination. In this chapter I discuss Karl Löwith's early reading of Nietzsche's *homo natura* as an example of philosophical anthropology (Löwith 1933). I take Löwith's essay to be among the first attempts to divorce the meaning of Nietzsche's *homo natura* from the neo-Kantian framework of its interpretation.

Löwith's approach to *homo natura* is not concerned with the theoretical question of positivistic naturalism (either in its natural scientific or historicist forms) but with the (philosophical) anthropological question of the whole nature of the human being. This is the same question which, according to Wolfgang Riedel, motivated literary anthropology at the turn of the twentieth century (Riedel 1996). Neo-Kantian accounts of Nietzsche's naturalism separate the question of *homo* from the question of *natura*, the practical from the theoretical strands of Nietzsche's philosophy. In contrast, the standpoints of philosophical and literary anthropology share the belief that one cannot separate the question of knowledge (of nature) from the question of how the human being ought to live because underlying both is the problem of self-knowledge of the human being as a living being, where the meaning of life can be captured neither in biologically reductionist terms (for example, genetics) nor in morally sublimated terms (for example, through a hierarchy of values or moral law).

The standpoint of philosophical anthropology offers some reasons why naturalistic interpretations of *homo natura* are too one-sided. First, due to an epistemological emphasis on *natura*, naturalistic readings run the risk of reducing the human being to a mere object of nature and as such miss the self-reflective dimension of knowledge. Second, they ascribe to Nietzsche a conception of nature that is largely drawn from the life sciences in the nineteenth century and as such do not sufficiently take into account the ancient Greek influence on Nietzsche's thinking about nature and life. Whereas in the nineteenth-century naturalist conceptions of life, nature denotes something that can be captured through scientific laws, Nietzsche held that for the Greek conception of nature, nature designates chaos. Nature as chaos is both inaccessible and indeterminable, creative and generative. To realise within the human being the extraordinary force of metamorphosis, of transformation and self-transformation – which is what I take to be the key point of Nietzsche's *homo natura* and of the task of translating the human being back into nature – the human being needs to recover nature's creative power of generation and creation of life.

This chapter defends Löwith's claim that the perspective of philosophical anthropology is needed in order to answer the question of the meaning of Nietzsche's enigmatic term *homo natura*. However, I argue that Löwith's overall account of human nature is too anthropocentric and does not adequately capture Nietzsche's conception of human life as continuous with the life of other living beings. Human nature in Nietzsche's philosophy of life exceeds the framework of a philosophical anthropology. Nietzsche rejects what Michel Foucault referred to as the anthropocentric turn in the nineteenth century (Foucault 1990a: 12). Therefore, a Nietzschean philosophical anthropology would have to consider the role of animal and plant life in Nietzsche's philosophy. These aspects of nature have in part been captured by literary anthropology. This chapter shows that what is creative and generative of culture in the human being is *natura*, the animal and plant life of the human being as a creative and generative source of metamorphosis, of human becoming and self-overcoming.

Karl Löwith and the Critique of Anti-natural Humanism

As far as I am aware, Löwith provides the first reading of *Beyond Good and Evil* 230 that explicitly links Nietzsche's conception of the human being as *homo natura* with philosophical anthropology.[1] In an article on Søren Kierkegaard and Nietzsche published in 1933, he advances the thesis that with Kierkegaard and Nietzsche philosophy becomes philosophical anthropology to the extent that all questions of philosophy are gathered up in one 'basic question (*Grundfrage*)': 'what is the human being?' For Löwith, Kierkegaard and Nietzsche address this question through two 'basic concepts (*Grundbegriffe*)': 'life' (Nietzsche) and 'existence' (Kierkegaard) (Löwith 1933). The main point of Löwith's philosophical anthropology, as I understand it, is that it moves beyond the Kantian dichotomy between the transcendental (*homo*) and the empirical (*natura*).[2] What distinguishes Nietzsche from Immanuel Kant is that *homo* does not transcend nature but is immanent to it. For the same reason, *natura* for Nietzsche is no longer simply an object of scientific enquiry but a force that exceeds human knowledge. When Nietzsche speaks of 'life', he means both the immanence of *homo* to *natura* and the excess of nature within the human being. Furthermore, whereas Kant's critical system seeks to define the conditions of possibility of knowledge which provide the critical foundation of the human and the natural sciences, with Kierkegaard and Nietzsche philosophy becomes philosophical anthropology in the form of an experimental psychology where truths are produced by the living philosopher's self-experimentations (ibid.: 43). Philosophical anthropology withdraws the ground of philosophy as the pursuit of absolute truth, but for Löwith this loss also announces a new beginning (ibid.: 46).[3]

According to Löwith, in Nietzsche, this new beginning arises from an overcoming of the Christian worldview and of its life-disdaining morality. Out of his critique of the Christian interpretation of human life, Nietzsche reconceives humanity as 'natural humanity' and the human being as *homo natura*. Löwith maintains that Nietzsche questions Christian morality on the basis of the distinction between what the human being *is* and what the human being *means*. Löwith illustrates this distinction by discussing the example of sinfulness: what sinfulness is for the human being and what it means for the human being as a Christian. The former denotes the 'natural being' of sinfulness, whereas the

45

latter denotes a 'moral' interpretation of what sinfulness is. This distinction does not coincide with the distinction between fact and mere interpretation, as naturalist readings of Nietzsche seem to suggest.[4] Rather it presupposes

> a natural conception (*natürlichen Begriff*) of the human being, of what is 'human (*menschlich*)' in the human being, because this human aspect is – in its own human way (*auf menschliche Weise*) – natural (*natürlich*). This natural humanity (*natürliche Menschlichkeit*) of the human being is ambiguously (*vieldeutig und unbestimmt*) referred to by Nietzsche as 'life'. (Ibid.: 59–60)

For Löwith, 'life' in Nietzsche is an 'ambiguous and indeterminate' term for the 'natural humanity (*natürliche Menschlichkeit*)' of the human being. Life is not reducible to biological or organic life, as in naturalist interpretations of Nietzsche, where nature is understood as an empirical given that can be accounted for by the discourses of the natural sciences.[5] This is why answering the question of human nature in Nietzsche requires a philosophical anthropology instead of a theory of knowledge. From the perspective of philosophical anthropology, 'life' can only be conceived of within the horizon of the human being's lived experience in the world. Furthermore, knowledge of the natural world, including the naturalness of the human being, can only be produced within the horizon of the human being's self-understanding, including its self-understanding as a natural being. This may explain why Löwith refers to 'life', 'human', 'nature' and 'natural' in quotation marks, indicating that these concepts are constructs of the human being's lived experience in the world. Löwith argues that for these reasons, sinfulness is not a phenomenon of the natural life or natural world. Instead, sinfulness only exists as a state of consciousness, as consciousness of sinfulness, which is why there are different possible ways of interpreting suffering.

In contrast to Christian interpretations of human life, the naturalised human being, as Nietzsche envisages it, no longer asks for the 'Why?' of its life and suffering:

> He does not only forgo 'reason (*Grund*)' but also 'meaning (*Sinn*)' and more generally 'interpretation' as the explication and exegesis (*Einlegung und Auslegung*) of meaning. He renounces them, because he has understood that objectively speaking the so-called meaning of human existence does not 'exist (*vorhanden*)'. Meaning exists only in accordance with what the human being means to himself (*was sich der Mensch bedeuten will*). (ibid.: 60)[6]

This new positioning of human nature 'beyond good and evil', beyond praise and reproach, calls for an affirmation of life and the love of fate expressed in Nietzsche's vision of the eternal recurrence of the same. For Löwith, the eternal recurrence of the same places the human being back into the eternal cycle of nature and thus constitutes the final step in the 'naturalisation (*Vernatürlichung*)' of morality (KSA 12:9[8]). When Löwith speaks of the 'eternal cycle of nature', he is not referring to the 'natural world' as it is construed by the natural sciences and its ideals of lawfulness, causation and so on. Note that for Nietzsche, there are no laws in nature: 'Let us beware of saying that there are laws in nature. There are only necessities' (GS 109). In the context of this aphorism, necessity in nature does not imply a deterministic worldview. Rather, necessity means that nature is anarchic: 'there is no one who commands, no one who obeys, no one who transgresses' (GS 109).[7] This is why necessity in Nietzsche is liberating the human being from deterministic and fatalistic conceptions of nature rather than underpinning them.

For Nietzsche, the naturalisation of morality, as with that of history, presupposes the de-deification of nature: 'When will all those shadows of god no longer darken us? When will we have completely de-deified nature! When may we begin to naturalize humanity with a pure, newly discovered, newly redeemed nature!' (GS 109). Löwith understands this call for a 'de-deified nature' as an absence of meaning (*Sinn*), a lack of order and determination (*Bedeutung*). Therefore, I take nature as 'meaninglessness of pure existence (*Sinnlosigkeit eines puren Daseins*)' in Löwith as an aspect of nature as chaos: 'Chaos sive Natura' (KSA 9:21[3]).[8] In my view, the liberation from the 'shackles of morality' does not occur through biological and psychological explanations of life.[9] What is liberating for the human being is the affirmation and love of nature as meaninglessness and anarchic chaos. Affirming and loving the meaninglessness of existence leads to a transformation of the human being: a sinful person becomes a sick person and a 'moral way of existence (*moralische Existenzverfassung*)' becomes a 'natural way of life (*natürliche Lebensverfassung*)' (Löwith 1933: 61).

However, for Löwith, Nietzsche leaves open the question of what is distinctly 'natural' for the human being and what distinguishes a 'natural' human life. Nietzsche's conception of *homo natura* and of the human being's 'naturalness' remains largely polemical, reactive and ultimately caught up within its opposition to the Christian moral worldview. Nietzsche sets out to decipher the 'eternal basic text of *homo natura*' behind the 'many vain and overly enthusiastic (*schwärmerischen*) interpretations and connotations (*Deutungen und Nebensinne*)' (BGE 230). However, Löwith concludes that he fails to reach a positive definition of human naturalness. Nietzsche's conception of human naturalness remains vague and indeterminate, oscillating between purely naturalistic and physiological explanations of the human and an articulation of a moralistic/immoralistic interpretation of the world.

Löwith laments that Nietzsche only gives a few historical examples of what he means by natural humanity: Greek antiquity and the human being in the Renaissance, as well as a few individual examples from modernity such as Goethe and Napoleon. But, for Löwith, these examples are not enough to provide a philosophical anthropology; they do not answer the question of human nature. Löwith regrets that 'Nietzsche did not discover a truly habitable "new land of the soul" on his "explorations of the nature of the human being"' (Löwith 1933: 64).[10]

In the final section of his text on Kierkegaard and Nietzsche, Löwith shares his own reflections on the human being's naturalness and the features of a future philosophical anthropology. He argues that when we ask what is 'human and in its own human way natural (*überhaupt menschlich und auf menschliche Weise natürlich*)', it would have to be something that is 'human in general (*allgemein menschlich*)' and 'natural' at the same time insofar as it would have to pertain to the 'general nature of the essence of the human being (*allgemeine Natur des Wesens des Menschen*)'. Löwith adds that the term 'general (*allgemein*)' would have to be understood historically, for the naturalness of the human being, as a human naturalness, is historical:

> Also the naturalness of the human being, has, as a human naturalness, its historicity (*Geschichtlichkeit*). What is natural to the human being, can only emerge (*hervorgehen*) and be understood on the ground of what the human being is in general (*was überhaupt menschlich ist*). (Ibid.: 64)

Although Löwith acknowledges that Nietzsche and Kierkegaard have opened the path for a new conception of the human being, the task of conclusively addressing the question of the naturalness of the human being now falls to a future philosophical anthropology.

Löwith ends his reading with a hint towards politics as an answer to the question of human nature and the general orientation of human life and existence. He notes that both Kierkegaard and Nietzsche end their writing careers on a political note: Kierkegaard invokes the rise of a 'divine world government (*göttliche Weltregierung*)' and Nietzsche announces the coming of 'great politics': 'with these political irruptions breaking out of their singular existence (*politischen Ausbrüchen aus ihrer Vereinzelung*), both authors demonstrate: the inner impossibility of a radically singular existence – before "God", or before "Nothingness"' (ibid.: 66). Shortly after Löwith, Hannah Arendt and Leo Strauss pick up these intuitions in Kierkegaard and Nietzsche in their own philosophical anthropologies, featuring politics as the distinguishing feature of human life in community with others (Arendt 1958; Strauss 1983). While I fully appreciate Löwith's assessment of the inconclusiveness of Nietzsche's philosophical anthropology by Löwith's own standards, there are good reasons why the question of the human being in Nietzsche remains open and why he does not provide a systematic philosophical anthropology.[11] I will further explore this aspect of Nietzsche's non–essentialist thinking about human nature as well as the political dimension of his philosophical anthropology in Chapter 4 and in the conclusion, arguing that Nietzsche's philosophical anthropology and his conception of *homo natura* is a variant of biopolitical posthumanism and provides the basis for an affirmative conception of a community of life between humans, animals, plants and other forms of life.

Recovering Animal Life

Nietzsche reconceives human nature from the perspective of a newly recovered Greek notion of nature, according to which animal and plant life are constitutive of human life. As such, Nietzsche's philosophical anthropology is distinctly anti-humanist (and posthumanist) insofar as it deconstructs the modern idea of a universe construed around the notion of the human being as a rational and moral agent.[12] Nietzsche's reference to the idea of *homo natura* as a 'basic text (*Grundtext*)' should therefore not be misunderstood as an example of 'anthropological absolutism'.[13] Rather, what Nietzsche uncovers behind the 'many vain and overly enthusiastic interpretations and connotations' (BGE 230) of human nature is the animality of the human being as the wellspring of its culture, and as what needs to be cultivated if the human being is to lead a 'more natural' human life.[14] Nietzsche maintains that the 'cruelty of the animal' is even active in the philosopher's pursuit of truth: the seekers of knowledge 'prevail (*walten*)' as 'artists and trans-figurers of cruelty' (BGE 229): '[I]n all desire to know there is a drop of cruelty' (BGE 229). Behind the humanist notion of the human being as a transcendental subject of knowledge, Nietzsche recovers the animality of the human being as the wellspring of its creativity: as the source of what is 'human and in its own human way natural (*überhaupt menschlich und auf menschliche Weise natürlich*)' in the human being, to employ Löwith's terms (Löwith 1933: 64).

51

It is important to point out that the conception of animality that Nietzsche adopts in *Beyond Good and Evil* 229 is neither produced through a Darwinian account of biological life nor by a consideration of the natural history of morals, where animality is simply what needs to be 'repressed' and 'disciplined' in order to make the human being apt for 'civilization' (Brusotti 2013). By way of contrast, Nietzsche attributes to animality a key role in his understanding of human culture as self-cultivation. According to Nietzsche's philosophy of culture, the cultural productivity of the human being derives from the cruelty of the animal. Culture in the human being is a thirst for 'the spicy potions of the great Circe, "cruelty"' (BGE 229). Circe is the goddess of metamorphosis. She has the power to transform the human being: '*Truth as Circe*. – Error has transformed animals into human beings; is truth perhaps capable of changing the human being back into an animal?' (HH 519). By invoking the truth of *homo natura*, Nietzsche seeks to transform the human being back into an animal that generates culture. This requires a transformation of our way of thinking about cruelty: 'Almost everything we call "higher culture" is based on the spiritualization of cruelty, on its becoming more profound – this is my proposition. That "savage beast" has not really been mortified, it lives and flourishes, it has merely become divine' (BGE 229).

According to Nietzsche, insight into the productivity of suffering is among the truths that have remained unsaid due to a 'fear of the wild cruel animal':

In late ages that may be proud of their humanity, so much fear remains, so much *superstitious* fear of the 'savage cruel beast', whose conquest is the very pride of those more humane ages, that even palpable truths remain unspoken for centuries, as if by some agreement, because they look as if they might reanimate that savage beast one has finally mortified. (BGE 229)

In these citations, Nietzsche places 'savage beast', 'savage cruel beast' and 'higher culture' in quotation marks, indicating that they are false ideas of human civilisation built on human prejudice and vanity. They are misconceptions grounded in a belief that the human being is something 'more' and 'higher' than nature, a belief that needs to be 'mastered'. Consider aphorism 230 in *Beyond Good and Evil*:

> To retranslate (*zurückübersetzen*) the human being back to nature; to become master over the many vain and overly enthusiastic interpretations and connotations that have so far been scrawled and painted over that eternal basic text *homo natura*; to see to it that the human being henceforth stands before the human being as even today, hardened in the discipline of science (*Zucht der Wissenschaft*), he stands before the rest of nature, with intrepid Oedipus eyes and sealed Odysseus ears, deaf to the siren songs of old metaphysical bird catchers who have been piping at him all too long: 'you are more, you are higher, you are of different origin!' (BGE 230)

For Nietzsche, depiction of the animal as 'savage' and 'cruel' participates in a larger strategy of domination and control whereby Christian morality seeks to establish the 'higher' distinction of humanity over and above its naturalness and animality. I would therefore agree with Löwith that Nietzsche's conception of the naturalness of the human being is an integral part of his more general critique of the Christian worldview and morality. But I add that it is the denial of animality (and, as I argue in Chapter 3, of the body) in Christian morality that Nietzsche hopes to overcome by means of a retranslation of the human being back into nature.

Laurence Lampert points out that Nietzsche contests the Christian denial of suffering as an essential aspect of life: 'Nietzsche advocates for suffering (cruelty) in an age where compassion and elimination of suffering are the highest goals of society and the state!' (Lampert 2001: 223). According to Lampert, 'cruelty belongs to our very nature as an animal species and needs to be enhanced for our species to be enhanced' (ibid.: 225). While I agree with Lampert on Nietzsche's critique of modern society and its hedonism, his reading of cruelty, which he equates with human suffering, remains anthropocentric. For Lampert, as for Marco Brusotti, animality only provides the raw material for the discipline and breeding of a higher human being. As such, this view acknowledges that animal cruelty plays a role in the natural history of morals but does not appreciate animality as a source of value in its own right. However, according to Nietzsche's philosophy of culture, 'cruelty' and 'suffering' are productive and need to be enhanced not because they preserve the human species but because they decentre the *anthropos* and as such enhance the transformative overcoming of the human being. In this sense, the naturalisation of the human being in Nietzsche reflects a move beyond both humanism and anthropocentrism.

Nietzsche views superstition and fear as symptomatic of civilisation and its domination over animal life and nature. I take Nietzsche's reference to superstition and fear in *Beyond Good and Evil* 229 as a way of distancing himself from both the humanism and the scientism of the Enlightenment.[15] Nietzsche is well aware of the dialectic of Enlightenment and rejects its desire for knowledge at any price, for 'objective' truth. He recalls that the Greeks 'knew how to live: what is needed for that is to stop bravely at the surface, the fold, the skin' (GS Preface 4).

Accordingly, it is questionable that Nietzsche would take his inspiration for the conceptualisation of human nature entirely from the discourse of the life sciences of the nineteenth century. Instead, he wants to bring us back to the Greeks and their thinking about the naturalness of the human being to open a new thinking about the nature of the human being that is creative and transformative and directed towards future becomings.

Recovering Nature as Art

Nietzsche's recovery of a Greek conception of nature as 'chaos' and characterised by the revaluation of 'animal cruelty' can be contextualised by placing it within the shifting significance of human nature in literary anthropology at the turn of the twentieth century (Riedel 1996). The reference to this *literary* background of Nietzsche's naturalism seems to be warranted by the fact that Nietzsche speaks of the '*terrible* basic text (*schreckliche Grundtext*)' that is *homo natura*. Furthermore, Nietzsche's access to this 'basic text (*Grundtext*)' seems to be mediated, as I shall discuss below, by his interpretation of Greek myth and tragedy. However, for Nietzsche these literary products are not expressions of a particular *human* civilisation that is ranked above others (as is typical for classicism). Rather, their significance is due to their being expressive of what lies at the origin or 'basis (*Grund*)' of human culture, namely, animal and plant life.

According to Wolfgang Riedel, the literary modernism of the nineteenth and early twentieth centuries arises from a paradigm shift in literary anthropology that reflects a new configuration between the philosophy of nature, biology and anthropology. Central to this paradigm shift is the concept of nature. The conceptualisation of nature in the nineteenth century assumed great anthropological relevance insofar as it led to an immediate reconceptualisation of the nature of the human being. According to Riedel, the main symptom of this transformation was a conceptual shift from 'nature' to 'life' (ibid.: viii–ix). This conceptual shift confirms the point of Löwith's philosophical anthropology, namely, that in Nietzsche natural philosophy (*Naturphilosophie*) becomes philosophy of life (*Lebensphilosophie*).

Riedel attributes this conceptual shift from nature to life to the rise of biology as the new episteme of nature.[16] But literary modernism and its reconceptualisation of human nature does not stand under the sign of an alliance between literature and biology. Instead, for Riedel this development expresses a new alliance between literature and natural philosophy: when the idea of nature found in the natural sciences was absorbed by literature it was transformed into the idea of 'the whole of nature (*ganze Natur*)' (ibid.: xii). In other words, the scientific idea of nature was appropriated by literature through natural philosophy. It is thanks to this alliance between literature and philosophy that literary modernism – and, I would add, philosophical anthropology – was able to preserve a non-scientistic idea of (human) nature.

Riedel traces this new conception of nature in literary anthropology back to Arthur Schopenhauer's philosophy of the will, which explains why its notion of nature is also non-idealistic:

> Schopenhauer's philosophy of nature sheds light on the double difference that separates the poetic conceptions of nature in literary modernism from contemporaneous conceptions of nature in the natural sciences (*Naturwissenschaft*), as well as from conceptions of nature in natural philosophy (*Naturphilosophie*) and literature found around 1800. (Ibid.: xv)

Riedel contextualises Nietzsche's *homo natura* within this larger paradigm shift towards a non-scientistic and non-idealistic understanding of the nature of the human being. In Nietzsche the 'intertwined thinking of biological anthropology and sentimental history of philosophy' (ibid.: 193) stands under the name of the Greek god Dionysus: 'the cult of fertility in the early Greeks' exemplifying a 'genuine and more natural humanity' (ibid.: 186).[17]

The ancient Greek idea of 'natural humanity' derives from a notion of nature as the basis of human culture.[18] In the Greeks, Nietzsche could easily find evidence for the belief that the human being is *homo natura*, a being whose culture is immanent to nature. Nietzsche first articulates this idea of nature as culture (and art) in the opening passage of *Homer's Contest*:

> The human being, in his highest, finest powers, is all nature and carries nature's uncanny dual character in itself. Those capacities of it that are terrible and are viewed as inhuman are perhaps, indeed, the fertile soil from which alone all humanity, in feelings, deeds and works, can grow forth. (HC)

For Nietzsche, human culture is immanent to nature to the extent that the human being's so-called 'natural' and 'human' characteristics are bound together to the point of indistinction. He understands the cultural achievements of humanity as rooted in the naturalness of the human being. What some humans take to be inhumane and terrible is in fact the 'fertile' growing ground of humanity. The reversal of the meaning of nature as 'terrible (*furchtbar*)' into 'fertile (*fruchtbar*)' allows Nietzsche to reaffirm with the Greek example that nature is an artistic and creative source of the becoming of culture. For Nietzsche the Greeks herald a genuine and natural humanity, the antipodes of humanity in the moderns: 'Thus the Greeks, the most humane people of ancient time, have a trait of cruelty, of tiger-like pleasure in destruction, in them . . . which . . . must strike fear into us when we approach them with the emasculated concept of modern humanity' (HC).

In *The Birth of Tragedy*, Nietzsche articulates the uncanny dual character of nature through the opposition between the Apollonian and the Dionysian impulses, which reflect the 'artistic double drive in nature' (BT 6):

> Thus far we have considered the Apollonian and its opposite, the Dionysian, as artistic energies (*künstlerische Mächte*) which burst forth from nature itself, without the mediation of the human artist (*Vermittelung des menschlichen Künstlers*) – energies in which nature's art impulses (*Kunsttriebe*) are satisfied in the most immediate and direct way: – first in the image world of dreams (*Bilderwelt des Traumes*), whose completeness (*Vollkommenheit*) is not dependent upon the intellectual attitude or the artistic culture of any single individual; and then as intoxicated reality (*rauschvolle Wirklichkeit*) which likewise does not head the single individual (*Einzelnen*), but even seeks to destroy the individual and redeem it by a mystic feeling of oneness. With reference to these immediate art-states of nature (*unmittelbaren Kunstzuständen der Natur*), every artist is an 'imitator' (*Nachahmer*), that is to say, either an Apollinian artist in dreams (*apollinischer Traumkünstler*), or a Dionysian artist in ecstasies (*dionysischer Rauschkünstler*), or finally – as for example in Greek tragedy – at once artist in both dreams and ecstasies [. . .]. (BT 2)

The Greek conception of nature is privileged by Nietzsche only because it confirms the more 'general' point that nature is artistic and that only by imitating nature, that is, by living according to nature (as exemplified by the Cynics), can the human being become again creative and cultured in its own terms.

In *The Birth of Tragedy*, there is a first formulation of the cruelty of nature. Nietzsche invokes the Hellene, 'by nature profound and uniquely capable of the most exquisite and most severe suffering' who has seen the 'cruelty of nature': 'Art saves him, and through art life saves him – for itself' (BT 7):

> With this chorus the profound Hellene, uniquely susceptible to the tenderest and deepest suffering, comforts himself, having looked boldly right into the terrible destructiveness (*furchtbare Vernichtungstreiben*) of so-called world history as well as the cruelty of nature (*Grausamkeit der Natur*), and being in danger of longing for a Buddhistic negation of the will. Art saves him and through art – life (*Ihn rettet die Kunst, und durch die Kunst rettet ihn sich – das Leben*). (BT 7)

The Greeks, as Nietzsche imagines them, are *homo natura*, with the Cynics and Diogenes of Sinope as perhaps the most radical example of a successful retranslation of the human being back into nature. On Nietzsche's early interpretation, Greek culture celebrates the naturalness of humanity, and hence they can release their suffering from the 'fearful, destructive havoc' in art (BT 7). This is not so for the 'Europeans of the day after tomorrow' (BGE 214) and the 'free spirits' (BGE 230) that Nietzsche addresses, who according to him live in an age of cultural decline and decadence produced by two thousand years of Christianity faced with the task of creating again a culture that overcomes the disdain of life inherent to Christian morality and civilisation.

Nietzsche distinguishes between two different types of suffering from life. The suffering he identifies in Greek myth and tragedy is a suffering from the fullness and overabundance of life that is discharged by generating culture. Nietzsche contrasts this affirmative conception of suffering from a modern kind of suffering that results from a lack of life which is impotent and unproductive. When Nietzsche calls for a rethinking of cruelty in *Beyond Good and Evil* 230, he is advocating for the former rather than for the latter type of suffering.

Löwith accuses Nietzsche of providing a conception of *homo natura* that is too polemical and too reactive, both by way of an overly enthusiastic affirmation of the greatness of Greek culture, on the one hand, and an overly critical stance against Christianity, on the other. For Löwith, then, this conception fails to articulate a more 'general (*allgemein*)' standpoint on 'natural humanity'. Against Löwith, one could argue that in *Beyond Good and Evil* 230 Nietzsche does put forward a 'general' claim about what is 'natural' in the human being, namely its drive towards knowledge and self-overcoming. In *Beyond Good and Evil* 230, this overcoming takes the form of an overcoming of civilisational conceptions of human nature. In the 'natural' human being, the 'basic will of the spirit', 'which unceasingly strives for the apparent and superficial' (BGE 229), is overcome by the opposite drive towards knowledge (*Erkenntnis*), the will to truth. Nietzsche's 'free spirits' turn the cruelty of the animal against themselves, the will to truth against the will to life, in the faith that the truth they discover may perhaps be 'capable of changing the human being back into an animal' (HH 519). Only thus can they unleash the transformative and regenerative forces of nature so that the human being can become again a creator and artist of life and inaugurate an age of cultural renewal. Culture in Nietzsche does not imply an overcoming of the 'wild cruel animal'. Instead, it requires an overcoming of the belief in the human being's distinction over and above nature and the animal. Insight into the nature of the human being as *homo natura* leads to a transformation of what the human being has become in the process of its civilisation rather than of the animal it is.[19] This is an important point, suggesting that what needs cultural transformation in the human being is not its naturalness and animality but rather the 'second nature' acquired in the process of its civilisation and so-called 'humanization (*Vermenschung*)' (BGE 242) that Nietzsche associates with Christianity and religion more broadly speaking (TI 'Improvers').

Recovering Plant Life

Against the background of Nietzsche's philosophy of culture and animality, Löwith's idea of the 'naturalness' of the human being appears too humanistic and anthropocentric. Löwith's account of Nietzsche's philosophical anthropology needs to be complemented by an affirmation of animality which encompasses the cultural value Nietzsche attributes to the animality of the human being. However, there is yet another form of non-human life at stake in Nietzsche's conception of the human being as *homo natura*: namely, plant life and the idea of the human being as a plant. Note the double meaning of '*zurückübersetzen*' in German as both 'retranslation' and 'replantation': *Beyond Good and Evil* 230 uncovers not only the human being's animality but also its vegetality. Throughout *Beyond Good and Evil* Nietzsche speaks of the human being not only as an animal but also as the 'human plant' (BGE 44), a plant that has been uprooted from its natural growing ground.[20] Nietzsche assigns to future philosophers the challenging task of reproducing the conditions under which the plant human being has so far grown furthest and highest (BGE 44). Retranslating the human being back into nature, then, not only means discovering and recovering the human being's animality, its instincts and natural drives, from which it has been alienated, but also replanting the plant human being into its 'natural' soil, from which it has been uprooted by processes of civilisation.[21] Hence, Nietzsche needs to be acknowledged at the forefront of those thinkers who seek to overcome, as Michael Marder puts it, the 'barriers that humans have erected between themselves and plants' (Marder 2013: 5).

As far as I am aware, the double meaning of '*zurückübersetzen*' as both 'retranslation' and 'replantation' has so far not been noted in discussions on the meaning of *homo natura* in Nietzsche scholarship. Rather, the emphasis has largely been on the textual metaphoric of aphorism 230, in which deciphering the 'basic text *homo natura*' is compared to interpreting a palimpsest.[22] Interestingly, in the French edition of *Beyond Good and Evil*, the sentence '*Den Menschen nähmlich zurückübersetzen in die Natur*' (BGE 230) is translated as '*Retransplanter l'homme dans la nature*' (cited in Kofman 1983: 135). Unfortunately, Sarah Kofman, who cites this passage at length, does not pick up this nuance in the French translation – an ironic lapse given her insistence on the primacy of interpretation in the Nietzschean *homo natura*. According to Kofman, with *homo natura* Nietzsche is not positing an original text of being or truth that is independent of interpretation.[23] Complementary with Kofman's reading, I argue that in order to fully appreciate the meaning of will to power as an art of interpretation, we need to acknowledge the transformative force of plant life within the human being.

In *Beyond Good and Evil* 230, Nietzsche makes a general claim about what is natural in humanity in relation to drives of knowledge which he here refers to as the 'basic will of the spirit

(*Grundwillen des Geistes*)'. The capacity of incorporation features as one of the main attributes of this 'basic' form of the will:

> The spirit's power to appropriate the foreign stands revealed in its inclination to assimilate the new to the old, to simplify the manifold, and to overlook or repulse whatever is totally contradictory – just as it involuntarily emphasizes certain features and lines in what is foreign, in every piece of the 'external world', retouching and falsifying the whole to suit itself. Its intent in all this is to incorporate new 'experiences', to file new things in old files – growth, in a word or more precisely, the *feeling* of growth, the feeling of increased power. An apparently opposite drive serves this same will: a sudden erupting decision in favour of ignorance, of deliberate exclusion, a shutting of one's windows, an internal No to this or that thing, a refusal to let things approach, a kind of state of defence against much that is knowable [. . .] all of which is necessary in proportion to a spirit's power to appropriate, its 'digestive capacity', to speak metaphorically – and actually, 'the spirit' is relatively most similar to a stomach. (BGE 230)[24]

The above passage offers an account of the human being's relation to its environment that is based on two opposed drives: a drive to master the environment by means of a dominating incorporation oriented towards growth and increased strength, and a drive to ignorance as a means of protection and preservation.[25] Nietzsche insists that these drives pertain to all beings that live, grow and reproduce themselves. Nietzsche compares the functioning of these two opposed drives and their relation to their environment to the digestive metabolism, and concludes that as such the 'spirit' is relatively most similar to a 'stomach' (BGE 230). I read Nietzsche's comparison of 'spirit' to 'stomach' in aphorism 230 within the context of his more general emphasis on the centrality of key attributes of plant life – nutrition, growth and reproduction – in his thinking about the human being.

Since Aristotle, the three key attributes of the 'basic will of the spirit', namely, the acts of nutrition (incorporation), growth and generation, are associated with the life of plants (Marder 2013). These same attributes are also central to Nietzsche's understanding of life as will to power: 'suppose all organic functions could be traced back to this will to power and one could also find in it the solution to the problem of procreation and nourishment' (BGE 36). In a posthumously published note, Nietzsche calls life 'a multiplicity of forces linked to each other through a common process of nutrition' and adds that 'everything we call feeling, representation and thinking' is part of this more general 'process of nutrition' (KSA 10:24[14]). On Nietzsche's hypothesis of the will to power, all higher organisms and psychic processes have thus never really superseded the 'basic *modus operandi* of the plant-soul': even in our highest endeavours, in the pursuit of truth, the human being remains a sublimated plant (Marder 2013: 40).[26]

Nietzsche then shows how the attributes of plant life manifest themselves in the human being. Just as in his explanation of the 'basic will of the spirit' in aphorism 230, he claims that the metabolic processes in the human being manifest themselves as a drive to create forms: 'the human being is a form-giving (*formenbildendes*) creature . . . When you close your eyes, you discover that a form-giving drive is continuously active within the human being, and that it tries out an infinite number of things that do not correspond to anything real' (KSA 10:24[14]). The creativity of drives in Nietzsche resonates with the theme of life as a dream in Nietzsche (D119 and 312, HH 13 among others). For Nietzsche, dreaming is a basic drive of all living beings, to the extent that to be alive means to continuously create, form and transform the nature of all living being. Both *topoi* depict the human being as traversed by nature's dreaming.[27] Nietzsche continues that '[t]he human being is a rhythm-giving (*rhythmen-bildendes*) creature' (KSA 10:24[14]). The form-giving process of nutrition and incorporation in the human being follows a rhythm, as in aphorism 230, between the will to master the environment through incorporation and the will to ignorance through non-incorporation. In *Beyond Good and Evil* 230, Nietzsche claims that the human being's inclination towards knowledge (*Erkenntnis*) is opposed to these two basic tendencies of all living beings, to either appropriate or to ignore, insofar as they are both falsifying:

> *This* will to mere appearance, to simplification, to masks, to cloaks, in short, to the surface [. . .] is *countered* by that sublime inclination of the seeker after knowledge (*Erkennenden*) who insists on profundity, multiplicity and thoroughness, with a *will* which is a kind of cruelty of the intellectual conscience and taste. Every courageous thinker will recognize this in himself [. . .]. (BGE 230)

However, the fact that the will to knowledge (*Erkenntnis*) is opposed to the two basic tendencies of life does not make this drive unnatural or anti-natural.[28] On the contrary, Nietzsche maintains that the metabolic processes of nutrition and reproduction manifest themselves in the human being as a 'resisting (*widerstrebende*) force': 'The human being is a resisting force' and 'knowledge . . . a means of nourishment' (KSA 10:24[14]). From the perspective of plant life, the drive to knowledge reflects the human being's drive to incorporate, grow and reproduce.

However, Nietzsche distinguishes between two types of nutrition: that which simply preserves us and that which transforms us. The same distinction applies to knowledge and the process of learning: 'Learning changes us; it does what all nourishment does which also does not merely "preserve" – as physiologists know' (BGE 231). From the perspective of plant life, transplanting the human back into nature produces a type of nutritive knowledge which has transformational power and is future-oriented. This is what I take to be the key message that Nietzsche directs to future philosophers confronted with the question of '"why have knowledge at all?"' (BGE 230).[29]

The transformative and regenerative power of plant nature also distinguishes an earlier aphorism in *Human, All Too Human*. In aphorism 107, Nietzsche offers a first comparison of human life with the growth and transformation of plants, anticipating the passage in *Beyond Good and Evil* 230 where Nietzsche compels the 'free spirits' to stand before the human being 'as even today, hardened in the discipline of science, he stands before the *rest* (*andere*) of nature' (BGE 230). In *Human, All Too Human* 107, Nietzsche maintains that '[a]s he [the human being] loves a fine work of art but does not praise it since it can do nothing for itself, as he stands before the plants, so must he stand before the actions of the human being'. In other texts, the point of Nietzsche's comparison is to show that the human being is not more than nature and does not derive from a higher nature-transcending origin.

> The complete unaccountability (*Unverantwortlichkeit*) of the human being for its actions and its nature (*Wesen*) is the bitterest draught the seeker of knowledge has to swallow, when it has been accustomed to seeing in accountability (*Verantwortlichkeit*) and duty (*Pflicht*) the patent (*Adelsbrief*) of its humanity (*Menschenthums*). (HH 107)

The conception of the human being as plant offends the human being's pride and vanity in its higher distinction, or what Sigmund Freud also refers to as the three 'offenses against human narcissism'.[30] Nietzsche's aphorism 107 nicely captures Freud's insight:

> It is the individual's sole desire for self-enjoyment (*Selbstgenuss*) (together with the fear of losing it) which gratifies itself in every instance, let a human being (*Mensch*) act as it can, that is, as it must: whether its deeds be those of vanity, revenge, pleasure, utility, malice, cunning, or those of sacrifice, compassion, knowledge. (HH 107)

Nietzsche is well aware of the difficulty of coming to terms with this new insight into human nature and offers the consolation that this knowledge (*Erkenntnis*) has a transformative and regenerative power:[31]

> Such pains are birth-pangs. The butterfly wants to get out of its cocoon, it tears at it, it breaks it open: then it is blinded and confused by the unfamiliar light, the realm of freedom. It is in such human beings that are capable of suffering (*Traurigkeit*) – how few will there be! – that the first attempt will be made to see whether humanity could transform itself from a moral to a wise humanity. (HH 107)

As in aphorism 230, this transformation requires a transplantation of the human being back into nature. It requires 'planting' new habits of evaluation that come to their full fruition under the influence of 'growing knowledge' which Nietzsche associates with the wisdom of a more natural humanity (HH 107).

In his writings, Nietzsche emphasises that 'transplantation' can be both transformative and healing. Nietzsche distinguishes between two types of transplantation (*Verpflanzung*): a 'thought-less change of location (*gedankenlose Verpflanzung*)' (HL 2) where a plant is 'alienated (*entfremdet*)' from its soil and then deterio-rates, and a 'change of location (*Verpflanzung*)' that functions as a 'spiritual and physical cure (*geistige und leibliche Verpflanzung als Heilmittel*)' capable of transforming the entire earth into a sum of 'places to recover health (*Gesundheitsstationen*)' (WS 188). Naturalist readings interpret Nietzsche's references to plant life as evidence for his naturalistic psychology.[32] Instead, the recovery of the metamorphic power of plant life allows Nietzsche to exemplify the transformative power of the pursuit of truth. Nietzsche invites us to re-evaluate truth from a post-Christian (im)moral perspective, a perspective that he associates with the wisdom of a more natural humanity. This perspective recovers the naturalness of the human being such that humans can transform themselves again into creators of new values and probe interpretations of the basic text *homo natura*.

Notes

1 This reading is distinct from that of Karl Jaspers, who understands anthro-pology as merely one aspect of Nietzsche's thinking about the human being (Jaspers 1981: 125).
2 For a similar point, see Heit (2014).
3 See also Jaspers (1981: 123–69); Schacht (2006: 116).
4 See Knobe and Leiter (2007).
5 See Leiter (1992).
6 Here, Löwith advances an indirect critique of Heidegger, who understands the being of humanity through the meaning-giving activity of existence.
7 On necessity in Nietzsche, see Siemens (2015).
8 On nature as chaos, see Babich (2001) and Granier (1977).
9 As in Leiter (2013: 582).

10 Whereas Löwith regrets that Nietzsche did not go far enough, Karsten Harries laments that he went too far: 'No longer another Columbus eager to discover a better Europe [. . .] Nietzsche now appears as a mad discoverer who, dreaming of a lost continent beneath the waves, begins to break apart the planks of his ship' (Harries 1988: 43). Harries argues that the term '*Grundtext*' in BGE 230 is an oxymoron: 'Is not a text necessarily a human product, a conjecture that falsely claims the authority of a *Grund*? Where can we find a *Grund* to speak to us as a text would, presenting our existence with a measure?' (ibid.). Paul van Tongeren (2014) offers a good point to complement this reading by arguing that where Nietzsche posits a '*Grundtext*' he should have embraced the tragic vision of an '*Abgrund*' (abyss) instead.

11 See Richard Howey's (1973) reading of will to power in Nietzsche from the perspective of philosophical anthropology.

12 I here rely on Rosi Braidotti's definition of posthumanism (Braidotti 2013: 13–54).

13 Sommer (2016: 650–1); Brusotti (2014: 129).

14 For culture and animality in Nietzsche, see Lemm (2009).

15 On Nietzsche's critique of the dialectic of Enlightenment, see Adorno and Horkheimer (2002: 44); Maurer (1990).

16 Perhaps Riedel's analysis of the shifting meaning of 'nature' and 'life' allows us to reconcile the false opposition between naturalist and postmodern readings of Nietzsche's *homo natura*. His analysis shows that both nineteenth-century life sciences and ancient Greek conceptions of nature need to be acknowledged as important influences on Nietzsche's thinking about human nature. This book by no means wishes to deny the important influence of nineteenth-century life sciences on Nietzsche's thinking about human nature. However, I thematise this influence within a biopolitical framework.

17 Riedel's interpretation of *homo natura* in Nietzsche can thus be read as a correction of both Nehamas's aestheticism (1987) and Leiter's anti-aestheticism (1992).

18 For a classic discussion of the literary and philosophical sources of Greek and Roman naturalism, see Lovejoy and Boas (1997).

19 I disagree with Jennifer Ham's (2004) argument that all that is required to recover animality is forgetfulness. This undermines the task of self-overcoming implied in retranslating the human being back into nature.

20 For a more extensive discussion of Nietzsche's philosophy of plants, see Lemm (2016b).

21 On the idea that religion originally has root in agriculture, see Sanford and Shiva (2012).

22 See for example Lampert (2001: 230); Sommer (2016: 651).

23 Christa Davis Acampora and Keith Ansell-Pearson endorse Sarah Kofman's reading, adding that therefore 'we would do better to read him [Nietzsche] as calling for psychological and philological probity when it comes to dealing with the many "vain" and "fanciful" interpretations that have been scrawled over the eternal basic text and which conceal their nature as such by masking the fact that the text, any text, is only what it is through interpretation' (Acampora and Ansell-Pearson 2011: 164–5).

24 Andreas Urs Sommer (2016) derives Nietzsche's conception of the spirit from Otto Liebmanns, *Zur Analyse der Wirklichkeit,* which depicts it as a plant interacting with its environment. Sommer also cites Andrea Orsucci's claim that BGE 230 must be read in the context of the discourse on contemporary biology and physiology (Orsucci 1996: 55–6). Furthermore, Sommer traces the comparison of incorporation and nutrition to Ludwig Feuerbach, who popularised the idea that human beings are what they eat (Sommer 2016: 653). However, Sommer does not link the discourses on contemporary biology and physiology that may have influenced Nietzsche's comparison of the spirit to a stomach, back to the Aristotelian definition of life, in particular, vegetative life as nutrition, growth and generation that may have also influenced Nietzsche's thinking of the human nature and the various comparisons of the human being to a plant found in BGE.

25 On the two movements of incorporation in Nietzsche, see Lemm (2013).

26 See also Jonas (2001) on metabolism and freedom.

27 Nietzsche's intuitions on the intimate relationship between dreams and human nature are subsequently confirmed by Freud. I will further discuss the affinities between Nietzsche and Freud's conceptions of *homo natura* in Chapter 3. On life as a dream, see also Foucault: 'In the dream, everything says "I", even the things and the animals, even objects distant and strange which populate the phantasmagoria. . . . To dream is not another way of experiencing another world, it is for the dreaming subject the radical way of experiencing its own world' (Foucault 1993: 59).

28 See Lampert (2001).

29 In the BGE chapter 'Our Virtues' Nietzsche speaks in the name of the 'Europeans of the day after tomorrow' (BGE 214) who may live up to the 'strange and insane task' of translating the human being back to nature. In an attempt to 'naturalize' his future readers, in GS, 'Joke, Cunning and

Revenge': Prelude in German Rhymes, Nietzsche jokingly recommends that his future readers must have 'strong teeth' and a 'good digestion' (54). They must have 'strong teeth' like beasts of prey and they must be like plants with a 'strong stomach'.

30 The cosmological through Copernicus, the biological through Darwin and the psychological through Freud showed that 'the ego is no longer master in its own house' (X: 355, as cited in Binswanger 1947: 188).

31 See also Nietzsche's conception of critical history (HL 2), where he offers a similar consolation.

32 Leiter (2002).

3

Psychoanalysis and the Deconstruction of Human Nature

In aphorism 14 of *The Antichrist*, Friedrich Nietzsche announces that he has 'changed (*umgelernt*)' his way of thinking about human nature and that he has 'placed the human being back among (*zurückgestellt*) the animals' (A 14). Recent scholarship reads this aphorism as evidence of Nietzsche's adherence to a naturalistic conception of human nature that is Darwinist and falls within the remit of the life sciences of the nineteenth century.[1] Within this biological and evolutionary discourse, natural history means the history of the biological evolution of forms of life. In contrast to this view, in this chapter I argue that by placing 'the human being back among the animals' Nietzsche does not intend to adopt a scientific conception of biological evolution to replace the historicism developed in the nineteenth century.[2] Rather, for him the renaturalisation of the human being goes hand in hand with a renaturalisation of history.[3] Nietzsche asks what difference the discovery of *homo natura* makes for our historical self-understanding. What do the 'return to nature' and the 'renaturalisation' of the human being mean for our understanding of history? My hypothesis is that Nietzsche pursues two possible answers to this question: first, the idea that the writing of a 'natural' history must take its evidence from the way history is written on the body, and not in terms of idealities. Second, such a 'natural' history reveals a conception of human nature that is essentially engaged in cultural (self-)transformation, and as such overcomes the false dichotomy between culture and nature, human and animal.

The first of these hypotheses was famously identified by Michel Foucault in his essay 'Nietzsche, Genealogy, History' (Foucault 1977). As is well known, in that text Foucault says that Nietzsche's contribution to the knowledge of history consists in having rejected the search for 'origins' and replaced it with the practice of genealogy, which sets out to discover the 'descent (*Herkunft*)' and 'emergence (*Entstehung*)' of discourses by shifting its attention to the body:

> The genealogist needs history to dispel the chimeras of the origin [. . .] He must be able to recognize the events of history, its jolts, its surprises, its unsteady victories and unpalatable defeats – the basis of all beginnings, atavisms, and heredities. Similarly, he must be able to diagnose the illnesses of the body, its conditions of weakness and strength, its breakdowns and resistances, to be in a position to judge philosophical discourse. History is the very body of becoming [*l'histoire, c'est le corps même du devenir*], with its moments of intensity, its lapses, its extended periods of feverish agitation, its fainting spells; and only a metaphysician would seek its soul in the distant ideality of the origin. (Ibid.: 144–5)

The genealogical approach to the question of origins presupposes that analogy between body and history in order to break open the metaphysical unity of the *Ursprung* (origin) into the two genealogical modes of *Entstehung* (emergence, '*émergence*') and *Herkunft* (descent, '*provenance*'). When history is written according to the modality of descent, it serves to show the contingency of every

73

attribution of essence or necessity to things, orders and values. Foucault assumes that the analysis of descent/*Herkunft* can show us the contingency of values because of its special relation to the body. *Herkunft* designates that aspect of 'historical beginnings' in which the connection between history and body is most significant:

> The body – and everything that touches it: diet, climate, soil – is the domain of the *Herkunft*. The body manifests the stigmata of past experience and also gives rise to desires, failings, and errors [. . .] The body is the inscribed surface of events (traced by language and dissolved by ideas), the locus of a dissociated self (adopting the illusion of a substantial unity), and a volume in perpetual disintegration. Genealogy, as an analysis of descent, is thus situated within the articulation of the body and history. Its task is to expose a body totally imprinted by history and the process of history's destruction of the body. (Ibid.: 148)

However, in 'Nietzsche, Genealogy, History', Foucault does not mention the problem of *homo natura*. Perhaps for this reason he does not tackle the second hypothesis concerned with the continuum between culture and nature, humanity and animality, in relation to the historical nature of the human being. In this chapter, I shall argue that it was not Foucault but the existential psychoanalyst Ludwig Binswanger who comes closest to addressing the relation between *homo natura* and a new conception of natural history beyond the dualism of culture and nature by relating the bodiliness of history to its presupposition in animal and plant life.

Interestingly, one of Foucault's important early texts is dedicated to Binswanger's approach to psychoanalysis and presents a sympathetic interpretation of it (Foucault 1993). As Chapter 1 discusses in relation to Kantian anthropology, Foucault claims that his own aim was 'to announce the first deterioration in European history of the anthropological and humanist episode that we have known during the nineteenth century' (Foucault 1994a: 502; 1996: 16) and to 'define a method of analysis purged of all anthropologism' (Foucault 1990a: 16; Han-Pile 2010: 133). Foucault seemed to think that he shared this aim with Binswanger's methodological approach in psychoanalysis. In his *Introduction to Ludwig Binswanger's 'Dream and Existence'*, Foucault suggests that he has found an example of how such an analysis could look in Binswanger's 'royal road' in contemporary anthropology (Foucault 1993: 32). At the beginning of his Introduction, Foucault provides the following preliminary definition of Binswanger's existential analysis:

[. . .] the human being is nothing but the actual and concrete content which ontology analyses as the transcendental structure of Dasein, of presence-to-the-world. Thus, this basic opposition to any science of human facts of the order of positive knowledge, experimental analysis and naturalistic reflection does not refer anthropology to some a priori form of philosophical speculation. The theme of enquiry is the human 'fact', if one understands by 'fact', not some objective sector of a natural universe, but the real content of an existence which is living itself and is experiencing itself, which recognizes itself or loses itself, in a world that is at once the plenitude of its own project and the 'element' of its situation. Anthropology may thus call itself a 'science of facts' by developing in rigorous fashion the existential content of presence-to-the world. To reject such an inquiry at first glance because it is neither philosophy nor psychology, because one cannot define it as either science or speculation, because it neither looks like positive knowledge nor provides the content of a priori cognition, is to ignore the basic meaning of the project. (Ibid.: 32)

In this chapter, I draw on Binswanger's consideration of human nature as *homo natura* in Nietzsche and Sigmund Freud in order to illustrate what Binswanger takes to be 'the basic meaning of the[ir] project': the reconstruction of 'the real content of an existence which is living itself' in and through its experience of embodiment and prior to any 'civilizational' distinction between humanity and animality. I propose a different reading of *The Antichrist* 14 that shows why Nietzsche's (and also Freud's) project of the renaturalisation of the human being does not reflect a conception of human nature that begins and ends with the natural scientific and non-historical view of nature. My thesis is that Nietzsche and Freud employ natural science to deconstruct the civilisational ideal of humanity as superior to animals and plants. Both Nietzsche and Freud, however, set aside natural science when it comes time to reconstruct human nature from out of its place among animals and plants because natural science is unable to account for what Binswanger calls the 'inner history of life (*innere Lebensgeschichte*)' and its cultural productivity (Binswanger 1947: 167). The 'inner history' of the human being's embodied existence becomes the key to understanding Nietzsche's idea of natural history.

Binswanger acknowledges that both Nietzsche and Freud adopt the viewpoint of the natural sciences in their investigation of human nature: Freud's *homo natura* is a 'truly natural scientific, biological-psychological idea' (ibid.: 166).[4] However, Binswanger also maintains that they do so in order to deconstruct the metaphysical, moral and religious conceptions of human nature. Hence, the viewpoint of the natural sciences is adopted for strategic reasons and not as an end in itself.[5] Binswanger insists on Nietzsche's and Freud's relentless efforts to dismantle the vanity and hypocrisy of the human being by uncovering *homo natura* beneath the civilisational constructs of *homo cultura* (ibid.: 161). For Binswanger, Nietzsche's and Freud's critique of civilisation is one of the key achievements and merits of their naturalism. The scientific deconstruction of the human as it is deployed in Nietzsche's critique of civilisation is what I take to be at stake in aphorism 14 of *The Antichrist*.

The discovery of *homo natura*, a newly discovered nature, entails the task of deconstructing history in order to take all teleology, theology and theodicy out of its occurrences. The goal of this deconstruction is to regain a 'more natural' conception of history (HL 10) that allows for a different and new self-understanding of the human being. I will discuss the key elements of Nietzsche's critique of civilisation and his deconstruction of history in the first part of this chapter.

Although Binswanger insists on the scientific nature of Freud's and Nietzsche's approach to the question of the human being, he is careful not to fall back into naturalistic and scientistic conceptions of human nature that treat the human being as an object of nature. When Binswanger insists that Freud's approach to human nature needs to be understood in strictly scientific terms and reflects the perspective of the natural scientist, or when Nietzsche invokes the 'discipline of science (*Zucht der Wissenschaft*)' in aphorism 230 of *Beyond Good and Evil* as the privileged vantage point of an investigation of human nature, this does not mean that Nietzsche and Freud are advancing some kind of 'anthropological absolutism' or reductionist naturalism.[6] Their approach to human nature is not rooted in the 'truth' of the natural sciences, as if one could explain how and why a certain type of person comes to bear certain values and ideas just as 'one might come to understand things about a certain type of tree by knowing its fruits' (Leiter

2002: 10). For Binswanger, Nietzsche and Freud investigate the 'inner history of life (*innere Lebensgeschichte*)', the history of the human being's embodied existence rather than the 'functionality (*Lebensfunktionen*)' of the empirical body (Binswanger 1947: 167). Nietzsche's and Freud's anthropologies are inspired by the discovery of the human being's bodiliness (*Leiblichkeit*) and vitality (*Vitalität*) as a living being (ibid.: 168). Nietzsche and Freud embrace Charles Darwin's revolution in biology insofar as they accept that an investigation of human nature needs to begin with the acceptance that the human being is an 'animal (*animalische Kreatur*)' (ibid.: 184). Binswanger extends this point also to the life of plants by drawing an interesting comparison between the scientific idea of the 'archaic plant (*Urpflanze*)' and Freud's idea of *homo natura*, two ideas that were designed to explain the productive nature of organic life (ibid.: 164). Binswanger approvingly cites Goethe's account of the metamorphosis of the plant as an analogy for his own reflections on the cultural transformations of human nature (ibid.: 178).

Binswanger distances Nietzsche's and Freud's consideration of the human being's bodiliness and vitality from scientistic and reductionist naturalism. Binswanger warns against the dangers of a naturalistic psychology which produces a one-sided image of the human being:

If the body (*Leib*) and its needs (*Bedürfnissen*) are the judges over (*Richterbefugnis*) the whole nature of the human being (*Ganze des Menschseins*), then the image of the human being (*Menschenbild*) becomes 'one-sided' and ontologically falsified. Then only what the human being is *as* a body, that is, what it experiences, feels, suffers, desires, is considered as real (*real*) and as true (*wirklich*). That is, what the human being feels 'in' and 'on' its body; what it perceives through its body and perhaps what it expresses 'with' its body (Klages). Everything else now inevitably becomes 'surplus (*Überbau*)', that is, 'fabrication (*Erdichtung*)' (Nietzsche), refinement (*Verfeinerung*) (sublimation) und illusion (Freud) or adversary (Klages). (Ibid.: 169)

In contrast to reductionist naturalism, Nietzsche and Freud situate the human body within the horizon of the human being's (self-)experience as a living being. This is an important aspect of Binswanger's understanding of human nature in Nietzsche and Freud that he shares with Karl Löwith's take on Nietzsche's philosophy as a philosophical anthropology. Both Löwith and Binswanger identify a naturalism in Nietzsche and in Freud that is centred on the question of the human being and its (self-) experience as a meaning-creating (Löwith) and culture-creating (Binswanger) living being. The philosophical idea of the body is an aspect of Nietzsche's and Freud's naturalism and their conceptions of natural history that is not captured in reductionist and scientistic accounts of *homo natura* and that I will discuss in the second part of this chapter.

For Nietzsche and Freud, the use of natural science is not sufficient to renaturalise the human being because for them the question of the human being's capacity for knowledge (*Erkenntnisfähigkeit*) does not exhaust the question about *homo natura*, as it is the case instead for Kantian epistemology. Binswanger would disagree with Brian Leiter's claim that with *homo natura* 'Nietzsche wants to establish a proper starting point for knowledge' (Leiter 1992: 279). For Binswanger, Nietzsche and Freud are primarily concerned with the human being's capacity for culture: 'for Freud the basic question (*Grundfrage*) is how far the cultural capacity of the human being extends' (Binswanger 1947: 163). The rigorous, scientific deconstruction of human nature and the importance both Nietzsche and Freud ascribe to an investigation of the human body are not the only distinguishing features of Nietzsche's and Freud's recovery of *homo natura*. Binswanger explains that the deconstruction of the human is not the end point of Freud's and Nietzsche's critique of civilisation. Rather, it prepares what they both refer to as the recovery of the naturalness of the human being. In Nietzsche's terms, this is the 'renaturalization (*Vernatürlichung*)' of the human being (GS 109; KSA 9:11[211]). Renaturalisation is at the heart of Nietzsche's and Freud's larger project of cultural renewal. It would therefore be false to assume that the end-product of the natural-scientific deconstruction of human nature already encapsulates Nietzsche's conception of the naturalness of the human being, as naturalist readings seem to suggest.

Renaturalisation in Nietzsche and Freud is diametrically opposed to the 'humanization (*Vermenschlichung*)' of the human being associated with the project of civilisation (BGE 242).[7] Addressing the question of renaturalisation relies on a theory of cultural productivity that exceeds the limits of scientific deconstruction and requires an interpretative, historical–philosophical reconstruction of human nature that I discuss in the third part of this chapter.[8] The challenge of such a reconstruction is not only to provide an understanding of who we are as human beings but, more importantly, to offer a vision of who else we could become. This is what I refer to as a transformational conception of natural history. Binswanger draws on Nietzsche's idea of the overhuman to illustrate this idea of human becoming that he finds absent in Freud.

In the final part of this chapter I suggest that Binswanger fails to appreciate the influence of the ancient Greek conception of nature on both Nietzsche's and Freud's thinking about human nature. Binswanger seems to be overly critical of Freud's theory of the drives that he wishes to complement with a philosophical idea of metamorphosis exemplified in Nietzsche's thinking about the *Übermensch*. Instead, I argue that Nietzsche and Freud rely on an archaic Greek conception of nature as chaos, according to which nature is a creative and artistic resource of transfiguration and transformation that cannot be fully captured by the discourses of the natural sciences.[9] On my hypothesis, *homo natura* in Nietzsche and Freud always already reflects an understanding of human nature that is engaged in cultural (self-)transformation and as such overcomes the dichotomy between culture and nature. Both Nietzsche and Freud advocate for a recovery of the human being's natural drives to overcome false conceptions of the human being produced by civilisation towards the cultivation of a more natural and genuine humanity. I take this transformational conception of natural history to be at the heart of their affirmative project of cultural renewal.

Deconstructing Human Nature through the Natural Sciences (A 14)

In his commemorative speech at the celebration of Freud's eightieth birthday, Binswanger uses Nietzsche's coinage *homo natura* to shed light on Freud's conception of human nature. Binswanger distinguishes between two different and consecutive steps in Freud's investigation of human nature: first, a rigorous-scientific deconstruction of human nature, and second, a creative-interpretative reconstruction of human nature. Whereas the first is an element in Freud's critique of civilisation, the second belongs to his larger project of cultural renewal.

Binswanger understands *homo natura* in Freud as the scientific idea of 'the human being as nature, as a natural creature (*als Natur, als natürliches Geschöpf*)' (Binswanger 1947: 159).[10] He remarks that Freud was the first to formulate a truly scientific theory of the human psyche analogous to a mathematical function of the soul.[11] The scientific method is employed by Freud, he suggests, for a deconstructive purpose:

> Nowhere is the destruction (*Destruktion*) of the human being more rigorous and thorough than in the natural science. Also, the natural-scientific idea of 'homo natura' must deconstruct (*destruieren*) the human being as a being that lives within a multiplicity of meaning direction (*in den mannigfachsten Bedeutungsrichtungen lebendes*) and that can only be understood out of this multiplicity of meaning directions. The natural-scientific dialectic must be applied to the human being until there remains only the product of tabula rasa, the dialectical product of reduction and everything that constitutes the human being as human and not only as an animal creature is extinguished. This must be and actually is the starting point for anyone who deals (*umgeht*) with the human being in practice or in science. (Ibid.: 184)

Binswanger adds in a footnote that Nietzsche followed the same method. When Nietzsche and Freud reduce the human being to its animal nature, this should not be misunderstood as scientistic reductionism. Rather, the objective of deconstruction is to reveal that all other things we find in life, namely sense (*Sinn*) and meaning (*Bedeutung*), are fiction (*Erdichtung*) or illusions or consolation, that is, beautiful appearance (*schöner Schein*) (ibid.: 185). For Binswanger, Nietzsche and Freud follow the method of the natural sciences by reducing the human being to a 'happening that bears meaning (*sinn-bares Geschehen*), to a being lived and overwhelmed (*ein Gelebt- und Übermächtigwerden*) by blind driving forces (*treibenden blinden Mächten*)' (ibid.). Binswanger explains that the point of their 'destructive-constructive method (*destructive-konstruktive Weise*)' is not 'to expose in an absolute sense the belief in meaning (*Sinnglaube*) as something that pertains to humanity (*Menschheit*) or to being human (*Menschsein als Ganzes*)' (ibid.), for that would be inherently nihilistic.[12] Instead, the great genius of Nietzsche and Freud was to unveil the hypocrisy of certain individuals, groups and cultural epochs, and not of humanity as a whole.

A reading of *The Antichrist* 14 illustrates how Nietzsche employs the viewpoint of the natural sciences to unveil a series of errors in the dominant conceptions of the human being found in the history of western civilisation. The discovery of *homo natura*, of the human being as a 'happening that bears meaning (*sinn-bares Geschehen*), a being lived and overwhelmed (*ein Gelebt- und Übermächtigwerden*) by blind driving forces (*treibenden blinden Mächten*)', requires that we rethink current conceptions of history that understand the human being as a historical agent. When one adopts the viewpoint of the natural scientist who stands before the human being as 'he stands before the *rest* (*anderen*) of nature' (BGE 230), one realises that humans are like animals and plants. It reveals that the agent of history is not the human being, but nature.

The Antichrist (14) begins with the following statement:

> We have learned better (*umgelernt*). We have become more modest in every respect. We no longer trace the origin of the human being in the 'spirit', in the 'divinity', we have placed him back among (*zurückgestellt*) the animals. (A 14)

The 'we' implied in aphorism 14 has gone through a process of transformation. In contrast to Nietzsche's 'free spirits' in *Beyond Good and Evil* 230, the group alluded to as 'we' in *The Antichrist*

14 is no longer stupefied before the 'terrible basic text of *homo natura*' (BGE 230). Those people have become masters over 'the many vain and overly enthusiastic interpretations and connotations that have so far been scrawled and painted over that eternal basic text *homo natura*' (BGE 230). The 'we' in aphorism 14 have undergone the 'discipline of science' and are 'deaf to the siren songs of the old metaphysical bird catchers who have been piping at him all too long: "you are more, you are higher, you are of a different origin!"' (BGE 230). They can say with confidence that the human being is not 'the great secret objective of animal evolution' and 'absolutely, not the crown of creation' and that all creatures of nature 'stand beside him [the human being] at the same stage of perfection' (A 14). As such, the seeker of knowledge finds a 'newly discovered, newly redeemed nature' (GS 109): for them nature is eternal and complete.[13] Nietzsche's philosophers dismantle history as teleology and as theology. For them, history is not the creation of a god, nor does it reflect the rationality or spirit of a higher human being. Furthermore, against the idea of historical progress, they discover that nature is eternal and always already complete.

Aphorism 14 of *The Antichrist* accomplishes this learning process and transformed perspective on human nature and history by systematically placing the human being back among the animals. As such, it illustrates Binswanger's account of the rigorous-scientific deconstruction of the human. In contra-position to *The Antichrist* 14, I read *Beyond Good and Evil* 230 as an interpretative historical-philosophical reconstruction of human nature that is comparable to the one Binswanger discovers in Freud. In the literature, both aphorisms are often cited together as evidence of Nietzsche's naturalism. At a closer look, however, both aphorisms offer a quite different treatment of the question of the nature of the human being. Whereas *The Antichrist* 14 enacts a 'tabula rasa' to reach the end product of a systematic deconstruction, Nietzsche's treatment of the naturalness of the human being in *Beyond Good and Evil* 230 is future-oriented and presents renaturalisation as the open task of retranslating and replanting the human being back into nature. Aphorism 230 ends in an *aporia* on the question of the value of truth and hints towards the transformative power of knowledge (*Erkenntnis*). As such, aphorism 230 has the features of what Binswanger refers to as the reconstruction of the naturalness of the human being in Freud.

In *The Antichrist* 14, Nietzsche does not adopt a forward-looking perspective that asks itself what else the human being could become by recovering the transformative power of nature. Instead, the aphorism adopts a backward-looking perspective at what the human being is, an animal among other animals. The opening passage confirms this point:

> We consider him the strongest animal because he is the most cunning: his spirituality is a consequence of this. On the other hand, we guard ourselves against a vanity which would like to find expression even here: the vanity that the human being is the great secret objective of animal evolution. The human being is absolutely not the crown of creation, every creature stands beside him at the same stage of perfection . . . And even in asserting that, we assert too much: the human being is, relatively speaking, the most unsuccessful (*missrathenste*) animal, the sickliest, the one most dangerously strayed from its instincts – with all that to be sure, the most interesting! (A 14)

The human being is distinct from other animals through its cunning and trickery, attributes that are symptomatic of the human being's vanity, an ongoing theme in Nietzsche and Freud.[14]

Nietzsche and Freud both diagnose an increasing sickness of the human being and agree that human civilisation has produced, as Nietzsche puts it, 'the most unsuccessful (*missrathenste*) animal, the sickliest, the one most dangerously strayed from its instincts' (A 14). In response to their diagnosis, they prescribe the healing effect of renaturalisation. They seek to recover the human being's natural health by means of philosophy as an art of transfiguration (Nietzsche) and psychoanalysis as an art of therapeutic transformation (Freud). Their aim is to initiate a renewal of culture by cultivating a natural and genuine humanity.

As such, the renaturalisation of the human being does not teach us who we are but who else we could become. Here, the problem connects to Leiter's account of Nietzsche's two projects, the theoretical and the therapeutical or practical, and his comparison of Nietzsche and Freud: Leiter reduces the retranslation of the human being into nature (BGE 230) (reconstruction) to the '*Zurückstellung* (placing back)' of the human being among the animals (A 14) (deconstruction), and thus misses the crucial difference between the two aphorisms and their treatment of the question of the human being.[15]

But the renaturalisation of the human being is not the actual topic of *The Antichrist* 14. Once sickness as the distinguishing feature of the human animal has been established, the aphorism proceeds to the actual deconstruction of the human. Aphorism 14 adopts the perspective of the past by recounting how our conceptions of human nature (metaphysical, moral, religious and so on) need to be reconceived following the rigorous application of insights derived from the natural sciences, including physics (mechanics), psychology, physiology, and so on. As such, the overall tone of *The Antichrist* 14 is misanthropic, concluding with the sobering 'dialectical product of scientific reduction' (Binswanger 1947: 184), the 'mortal frame' of the human being (A 14).[16] To reach this goal, Nietzsche takes his readers through the great errors in the history of philosophy from René Descartes to Georg Wilhelm Friedrich Hegel, revealing that at the heart of their anthropologies stand misconceptions of human nature. As such aphorism 14 accomplishes both a 'de-humanization (*Entmenschlichung*)' of nature and a de-deification of history.[17]

Nietzsche begins by inverting Descartes's philosophical method, which consists of a rigorous doubting of one's beliefs, ideas, thoughts and sensory experience in pursuit of the purity and veracity of spirit in form of the human cogito.[18] Nietzsche instead follows the logic of physiological proofs to take sides for and against Descartes:

> As regards the animals, Descartes was the first who, with boldness worthy of respect, ventured to think of the animal as a machine: our whole science of physiology is devoted to proving this proposition. Nor, logically, do we exclude the human being, as even Descartes did: our knowledge of the human being today is real knowledge precisely to the extent that it is knowledge of him as a machine. (A 14)

Nietzsche embraces Descartes's thesis that the animal (and hence also the human body) is a machine. However, he subsequently subverts it by confirming that, like animals, the human being is a machine: 'our whole science of physiology is devoted to proving this proposition' (A 14). Nietzsche's subversion of Descartes is a double reversal. First, he reverses Descartes's understanding of the human being as distinct from the animal by claiming that, from the point of view of physiology, there is no difference between animals and humans; and second, he subverts Descartes's understanding of the body as inferior to the mind by re-evaluating the status of the human spirit, claiming that it is only an (inferior) aspect of the body.

The second step in the placing of the human being back among the animals concerns the belief in the 'free will', the *liber arbitrium*, as the distinguishing feature of human nature:

> Formerly the human being was presented with 'free will' as a dowry from a higher order: today we have taken even will away from him, in the sense that will may no longer be understood as a faculty. The old word 'will' designates only a resultant, a kind of individual reaction which necessarily follows a host of partly contradictory, partly congruous stimuli – the will no longer 'effects' anything, no longer 'moves' anything. (A 14)

This time, Nietzsche employs the insights drawn from psychology against the errors in moral conceptions of the nature of the human being. Psychology shows that the Christian concept of 'free will' is in fact a multiplicity of drives and instincts that are irreducible to one another and lie at the basis of our so-called 'actions'. When one adopts the viewpoint of the natural scientist who stands before the human being as 'he stands before the *rest* (*anderen*) of nature' (BGE 230), one realises that humans are like animals and plants: they lack the freedom to act at will. Actions should therefore not be thought of as willed or as conscious (TI 'Errors' 7). According to Nietzsche, the Christian doctrine of the free will 'has been invented essentially for the purpose of punishment, that is, of *finding guilty*' (TI 'Errors' 7). Its ultimate purpose is to satisfy its authors' 'desire to create for themselves a *right* to ordain punishment – or their desire to create for God a right to do so . . .' (TI 'Errors' 7). Nietzsche insists that it is only because 'the human being *regards* itself as free, not because it is free, that it feels remorse and pangs of conscience' (HH 39). Against this doctrine,

Nietzsche puts forward the idea that 'everything is innocence' (HH 107 and TI 'Errors' 8). The point of Nietzsche's critique of the Christian doctrine of 'free will' is that its corresponding idea of moral responsibility fails to generate genuine responsibility. Instead, the human being needs to recover its animal innocence to recognise in an 'action compelled (*zwingt*) by the instinct of life' and carried out with 'joy' the 'right (*rechte*) action' (A 11). Freud confirms and complements Nietzsche's insights into the 'pleasure principle' with a theory of the drives which demonstrates that the will, or the Ego, is no longer 'the master of his household' (Binswanger 1947: 188). A note from Nietzsche's *Nachlass* summarises this point:

> The act of free will would be a miracle, a break in the chain of nature. The human beings would be miracle workers. The consciousness of a motive comes with an illusion – the intellect, the primordial (*uranfängliche*) and only liar. (KSA 8:42[3])

By placing the human being back among the animals and plants, Nietzsche closes the gap in the chain of nature and re-establishes the truth of nature: 'the intellect, the primordial (*uranfängliche*) and only liar' (KSA 8:42[3]).

The third and last step in Nietzsche's scientific reduction of the human being to the animal concerns the idea of the purity of the spirit. In contrast to the view that spirit is the sign of human distinction and elevation, Nietzsche employs the knowledge produced by modern biology to reveal that the spirit is nothing but 'a pure stupidity':[19]

> Formerly one saw in the human being's consciousness, in his 'spirit', the proof of his higher origin, his divinity; to make himself perfect, the human being was advised to draw his sense

back into himself in the manner of the tortoise, to cease to have any traffic with the earthly, to lay aside his mortal frame: then the chief part of it would remain behind, 'pure spirit'. We thought better of this too: becoming-conscious, 'spirit', is to us precisely a symptom of a relative imperfection of the organism, as an attempting, fumbling, blundering, as a toiling in which an unnecessarily large amount of nervous energy is expended, – we deny that anything can be made perfect so long as it is still conscious. 'Pure spirit' is pure stupidity: if we deduct the nervous system and the senses, the 'mortal frame', we miscalculate – that is all! (A 14)

The inferiority of the conscious over the unconscious is another common *topos* in Nietzschean and Freudian psychology. In *The Gay Science*, for example, Nietzsche maintains that contrary to the belief that consciousness denotes the human being's superiority with respect to other forms of life, consciousness in the human animal is a relatively young, insufficiently developed organ which, as such, can even be dangerous (GS 11, 354). Nietzsche re-establishes the value of the unconscious by reminding us that most of the human animal's vital functions operate without consciousness and that it is thanks to their unconsciousness rather than their consciousness that the human animal has so far preserved itself. Freud's theory of the unconscious will confirm this intuition in Nietzsche.

Despite Nietzsche's and Freud's sobering accounts of human consciousness as a secondary phenomenon in the life of the human psyche, neither of them simply gives up on consciousness altogether. As Binswanger points out, this would be a huge misunderstanding. Once Nietzsche and Freud have reached the 'dialectical product of scientific reduction' (Binswanger 1947: 184) – the 'mortal frame' of the human being (A 14) – the question becomes whether one can plant a different kind of consciousness that embraces the bodily (animal and plant) dimensions of human life as the growing ground of a natural humanity. This question leads Nietzsche and Freud to an investigation of the human being's bodiliness (*Leiblichkeit*) and vitality (*Vitalität*) as a living being (Binswanger 1947: 168).

A New Philosophy of the Body

Binswanger notes that the importance both Nietzsche and Freud ascribe to an investigation of the body is a distinguishing feature of their conception of human nature.[20] In particular, it sets their idea of *homo natura* apart from the romantic notion of a return to nature:

> Whereas the Rousseauian idea of *homo natura* is a cheering utopia of the angelical nature of the human being born from a benevolent nature, a *homo natura benignus et mirabilis* so to speak, the idea of *homo natura* in Novalis arises from a magic idealisation of bodiliness and a magic naturalisation of spirit, the *homo natura* in Nietzsche and Klages is based on the same idea as in Freud: here bodiliness (*Leiblichkeit*) determines what the human being is in its essence. (Binswanger 1947: 168)[21]

Nietzsche's recommendation to follow the 'guiding-thread of the body (*Leitfaden des Leibes*)' 'in all matters of scientific inquiry' (KSA 11:26[432]), especially those related to the spirit (KSA 11:26[374]; see also KSA 12:2[91]) confirms Binswanger's observation. A posthumous note thematises this new perspective in philosophy:

> If we assume that the 'soul' was an attractive and mysterious thought, a thought which philosophers rightfully only gave up reluctantly – maybe what they have learned to receive in

exchange for the 'soul' is something even more attractive, even more mysterious: the human body. The human body, in which the whole far and recent past of all organic becoming is again alive and corporal, through, above and beyond which a tremendous unheard stream seems to flow: the body is a much more remarkable thought than the old 'soul'. (KSA 11:36[35])[22]

There are three points I wish to make regarding this new perspective in philosophy. First, the above note illustrates that what fascinates Nietzsche (and, I would add, Freud) is not the empirical but the philosophical idea of the body: 'the body is a much more remarkable thought than the old "soul"' (KSA 11:36[35]). The key for Nietzsche is not only to understand that in the human body 'the whole far and recent past of all organic becoming is again alive and corporal' (KSA 11:36[35]) but also that 'the whole pre-history and past of all sentient being, continues within me [Nietzsche] to fabulate, to love, to hate, and to infer' (GS 54). Although Nietzsche acknowledges that the natural sciences are making an important contribution to an enhanced understanding of the human body, neither the insights they provide nor the methods they follow will answer the question of human nature, that is, of the inner historicity of life. Rather, explaining how 'the whole far and recent past of all organic becoming is again alive and corporal' (KSA 11:36[35]), and grasping how 'the whole pre-history and past of all sentient being, continues within me [Nietzsche] to fabulate, to love, to hate, and to infer' (GS 54), requires the imagination of the philosopher and poet who has ears for the 'tremendous unheard stream' that flows 'through, above and beyond' the human body (KSA 11:36[35]).[23] Nietzsche views the person like a natural organism, but the whole life of this natural organism cannot be made intelligible through the discourses of the natural sciences. It requires the discourse of a natural history. Naturalistic and reductionist accounts of the human body in Nietzsche miss this difference between the empirical body and the living body as a 'marvellous bringing together of the most multiple life' (KSA 11:37[4]) and therefore provide only a one-sided conception of human nature, of the human as a living and historical being, in Nietzsche.[24]

Second, both Nietzsche and Freud are well aware of the limits of their endeavours into human nature. Freud, for example, describes his attempts to capture human nature through a theory of the drives intended to grasp the meaning and origin of the human being's psychic life and its link with the 'archaic ground of all life (*Urgrund allen Lebens*)' (Binswanger 1947: 160) as a confronting, discomforting and uncanny experience which leads him to acknowledge the mythological nature of his own scientific endeavours:

> The theory of the drives is, so to say, our mythology. Drives are mythical entities, magnificent in their indefiniteness. In our work we cannot for a moment disregard them, yet we are never sure that we are seeing them clearly. (Freud 1933: 95, cited in Binswanger 1947: 160)[25]

Freud's 'apprehensive astonishment, his shivering before the "uncanny (*ungeheuren*) invisibility"' of the drives attests to the impossibility of discerning with certainty the truth of human nature (Binswanger 1947: 160). For Freud, the endeavours of the natural scientist are therefore inherently tragic in kind. There is no consolation before the violent force of nature and its immanent death, and hence Freud concludes that it must be the destiny of the human being to bear the suffering and pain inflicted by nature as 'the first duty of all living beings':

> The unremitting astonishment of the natural scientist before the seriousness and power of life and its immanent death, the astonishment before a life, of which Freud [and, I would add, Nietzsche] believed that it 'causes our suffering (*wir all schwer leiden*)' (XI, 464), for which there exists no compensation (ibid.) and no consolation, a life that we all have to bear as the 'first duty of all living beings'. (X 345 f.; Binswanger 1947: 160)[26]

Freud's tragic vision of life and his acknowledgement of the limits of human knowledge resonates with Nietzsche's philosophy. The impossibility of drawing a line between science and mythology is an ongoing theme in Nietzsche's work. Nietzsche draws the image of the human being as unaware of its being attached to the back of a tiger and claims that nature threw away the key to the mishmash of physiological activity in the body (TL). Nature manifests itself in and through the body as a wild, untamed and uncontrollable force that is indeterminate and inaccessible to human consciousness. This is an insight that no doubt complicates Nietzsche's and Freud's question of how to cultivate a different kind of consciousness and history that embraces the bodily (animal and plant) dimensions of human life as the growing ground of a natural humanity. Both Nietzsche and Freud acknowledge that their attempt to provide a natural history of human life fails insofar as the latter is strictly unintelligible and remains unknown. I will return to this aspect of the incompleteness or inherent failure of natural history in a moment.

The final point I make in regard to Nietzsche's and Freud's investigation of the human being as an embodied and living being is that this investigation is oriented towards an overcoming of the human. As Werner Stegmaier and Andrea Bertino (2015) have correctly pointed out, Nietzsche's (and, I would add, Freud's) anthropology is always also a critique of anthropology. Nietzsche and Freud rely on the discoveries of their contemporaries in the natural sciences to show that the human being is neither a rational nor a moral creature. Their underlying motivation is to overthrow dominant conceptions of the human being that can no longer be upheld as a result of scientific discoveries. A note from Nietzsche's *Nachlass* on the development of organic life illustrates this idea:

> Perhaps the whole development of the spirit concerns the body (*Leib*): it is the history of the formation of a higher body (*Leib*) that is becoming perceptible. The organic is ascending towards higher stages. Our craving for knowledge of nature is a means through which the body (*Leib*) strives to perfect itself. Or rather: hundreds of thousands of experiments in nutrition, dwelling and ways of living are to transform the body (*Leibes*): consciousness and valuation, all kinds of desires and lacks of enthusiasm are symptoms of these changes and experiments in the body. In the end it is not about the human being: it is about its overcoming. (KSA 10:24[17])[27]

This note shows that against the background of the development of organic life, human nature is not something that is absolute, stable and fixed. Rather, human nature is involved in the continuous formations and transformations of nature. Natural history is an open-ended history. From the perspective of the historical development of organic life, culture is not the distinguishing feature of the human being. Instead, culture and history are always already immanent to nature.

For Nietzsche and Freud, answering the question of how to plant a different kind of consciousness, how to conceive of a different historical narrative, that embraces the bodily dimensions of human life as the growing ground of a natural humanity, means to affirm nature as a creative and artistic force.[28] It requires an overcoming not of what the human being is, a natural creature, but of what it has become in the process of its civilisation. Again, how such a (self-)overcoming of the human can be conceived is a question that exceeds the limits of the natural sciences and requires a philosophical anthropology to provide an account of culture and history that does not transcend nature. This is what I take to be the purpose of Nietzsche's and Freud's reconstruction of human nature on the grounds of a 'de-deified' nature, a 'newly discovered, newly redeemed nature' (GS 109).[29]

Drives, Culture and Human Transformation

Marco Brusotti (2013) argues that aphorism 230 of *Beyond Good and Evil* reflects a 'natural history of the free spirit', which provides an account of the nature of the human being as *homo natura*. In this aphorism, Nietzsche explains the emergence of culture (and knowledge) from what he refers to as the 'basic will (*Grundwille*) of the spirit' (BGE 230) and adds that this 'basic will' pertains to all living beings. Commentators noted that this 'basic will of the spirit' has all the features of what Nietzsche otherwise refers to as the will to power (BGE 44) (Heit 2014). The underlying idea is that Nietzsche reconstructs human nature on the ground of his hypothesis of the will to power: '*Homo natura*. The will to power' (KSA 12: 2[131]).

Binswanger advances the same idea: a reconstruction of human nature must be based on a certain principle or idea, such as the idea of will to power in Nietzsche or the idea of the plea-sure principle in Freud. According to Binswanger, the idea of will to power in Nietzsche is 'to give meaning to the suffering of human life' (Binswanger 1947: 184). Likewise, the idea of the pleasure principle in Freud is 'to open the possibility for the preservation and enhancement of life' (ibid.). For Binswanger, this is the ultimate purpose of the reconstruction of human nature in Nietzsche and Freud. As such, Binswanger understands Nietzsche's idea of will to power as a special case of Freud's will to pleasure:

> Will to pleasure (*Lust*), i.e. will to 'life' and will to increase life (*Lebenssteigerung*) by letting be (*Gewährlassen*) the 'unknown, uncontrollable powers' through which the human being is lived (*gelebt wird*). (Ibid.: 170)

Both ideas – the will to power and the will to pleasure – offer an account of the nature of the human being that is both immanent to and exceeded by nature to the extent that the human being lives and is lived by and through nature: powers 'through which the human being is lived (*gelebt wird*)' (ibid.). At the same time, they make possible an account of human cultural productivity that does not rely on ideas of spirit or soul that transcend nature.

On this second point, Binswanger engages Nietzsche against Freud in the context of complementing a weakness he detects in Freud's thinking about the drives. For Binswanger, Freud's theory of the drives falls short of articulating an idea of human transformation. For Freud, the nature of the drives (*Triebwe-sen*) 'despite their multiple transformations ultimately remains unchanged', and hence Binswanger infers that 'in contraposition to Goethe and Nietzsche, Freud's doctrine of the drives does not articulate a genuine conception of transformation (*Wandlung*)' (ibid.: 178).

The critique voiced by Binswanger in his celebratory speech reflects a deeper, long-standing disagreement between Freud and Binswanger on the status of philosophy, in particular the status of Nietzsche's philosophy, in psychoanalysis.[30] While Binswanger agrees with Freud on the merits of his naturalism, he argues that the renaturalisation of the human being must involve 'more' than a theory of drives. He invokes the idea of the *Übermensch* in Nietzsche as an example of a philosophical-creative reconstruction of human nature that offers a more convincing account of human cultural productivity than Freud's (unphilosophical) scientific naturalism.[31]

Binswanger's mobilisation of Nietzsche against Freud on the question of the cultural metamorphoses of the human being has been questioned in the literature based on the textual evidence provided by a passage in *Beyond Good and Evil* 230, where Nietzsche explicitly states that the human being is not 'more' than nature (BGE 230) (Gasser 1997). On this view, Nietzsche would agree with Freud that the human being is not 'more' than the life of its drives. Interestingly, Freud's own reaction to Binswanger's speech points in a similar direction. In a letter to Binswanger, Freud writes:

> Of course, I do not believe you [Binswanger] nevertheless. I have always only spent my time in the main floor and basement (*Souterrain*) of the house. – You claim that when one changes the perspective, one can also see an upper level where the distinguished guests of religion, art, etc. live. You are not the only one who makes this claim; the majority of cultural exemplars of the *homo natura* think this way. In this respect you are conservative, and I am revolutionary. If I would still have

a working life ahead of me, then I dare say I would dedicate it to finding a living place for those who claim to be of a higher origin (*Hochgeborenen*) in the lower floors of the house. For religion, I have already found one when I encountered the category of 'neurosis'. But probably we simply do not understand each other and our disagreement will need a few hundred years to dissolve. (Cited by Gasser 1997: 235, my translation)

Like Nietzsche, Freud rejects theories of culture based on principles that transcend nature. Freud insists that there is nothing 'more' to the human being that would distinguish it from nature and other living beings. But does this mean that Freud's conception of human nature is entirely scientific, as Binswanger suggests? A different perspective on the notion of nature in Nietzsche and Freud may help to address Binswanger's concerns.

Chaos, Creativity and Becoming Overhuman

Jean Granier (1981) offers a different position on the relation between Nietzsche and Freud regarding the status of philosophy and the question of the nature of the human being that both contrasts with and complements Binswanger's point of view. According to Granier, the common terminology between Nietzsche and Freud – the terms *Es* and *homo natura* – suggests that Freud's conception of the human being as *homo natura* is essentially a philosophical one.[32] When Freud adopts the word *Es* coined by Nietzsche to designate the origin of the human being's psychic life, he does not merely adopt a word. Rather, the choice of words in Freud is based 'on a type of reflection that is philosophical in nature' (ibid.: 100, my translation). Likewise, the reference to *natura* in *homo natura* demonstrates that Freud's reflections on the question of the human being exceed by far the framework of his clinical experience and his socio-cultural investigations. Granier, like Binswanger, cites the passage in Freud where he acknowledges the mythological status of his theory of the drives (Binswanger 1947: 160; Freud 1933: 95; Granier 1981: 101). Granier insists that mythology for Freud is by no means an aggregate of illusions and phantasms. Instead, Freud explicitly reestablishes the power of mythology and of myth to reveal (*dévoilment*) truth.

Granier argues that Freud's conception of nature is in many ways comparable to that of Goethe and of the thinkers and artists of the Renaissance, such as Leonardo da Vinci.[33] Freud's way of speaking of nature reminds Granier of the 'distress and adoration the Greeks experienced before what they named *aidos*' and infers that mythology in Freud plays the same role as in the Greeks, namely 'a discourse on the origin, on the primordial' (Granier 1981: 101). For Granier, this mythic origin of psychic life represents nothing less than another name for being, for life in its totality, and hence he concludes that Freud's, like Nietzsche's, conception of the human being as *homo natura* is philosophical.

On Granier's account, when Nietzsche employs the term *natura* to determine human nature, the objective is neither to grasp the psychological life of the human being (as in Freud) nor to articulate a philosophical anthropology (as in Löwith). Rather, the point of Nietzsche's reconstruction of human nature as *homo natura* is to recover an archaic conception of nature as chaos: 'Chaos sive Natura' (KSA 9:21[3] and 9:11[197]) (Granier 1977). Nature as chaos designates an idea of nature as a creative and abundant force that brings forth life of and out of itself (Babich 2001).[34] It is by recovering this creative and artistic force of nature that Nietzsche hopes to unleash within the human being its potential for formation and transformation.

According to Granier, chaos is for Nietzsche the abyssal reality of being as will to power. In both Nietzsche and Freud, nature is featured as inaccessible to the human being referring it back to an origin, a ground (*Grund*) that reveals itself as abyss (*Abgrund*).[35] Here, Freud's and Nietzsche's reflections on the nature of the human being rejoin. On Granier's hypothesis, Freud conceives of the drives of the human being in the same way as Nietzsche conceives of nature, as chaos. Granier therefore concludes that, by borrowing the term *Es* from Nietzsche, Freud accomplishes the philosophical truth of his psychoanalytical reflections:

> If Nietzsche's and Freud's radical critique of civilization has revolutionized the nature of philosophy, this subversion does not conclude with the destruction (*destruction*) or annulation of philosophy. Rather it leads to an overcoming in the Nietzschean sense of the term *Überwindung*, that is, the reconversion (*reconversion*) of philosophy through a return to the origin that unveils being as something that lies beyond what can be demonstrated by objective reason and thus allows philosophy to reconquer its truth as a discourse of the world. (Granier 1981: 102)

Granier's use of the terms 'destruction' and 'reconversion' recalls the notions of deconstruction and reconstruction in Binswanger. However, for Granier, Freud's reconstruction of human nature is no less philosophical than that of Nietzsche. Binswanger and Granier pursue different objectives: to prepare the way for an anthropological–philosophical analysis of human existence in psychoanalysis (Binswanger) and to recover the truth of philosophy as a discourse on nature and the world beyond metaphysics (Granier). However, their reconstruction of Nietzsche's and Freud's anthropologies conclude on the same opening towards the future, that is, the transformation of the human being: the metamorphosis of the human being in Binswanger and the renewal of philosophy in Granier.

Nietzsche articulates this idea of future becoming through the emblematic image of the *Übermensch* where an overcoming of the human occurs in the name of animality as the human being's eternal source of self-transformation. The *über* in Nietzsche's *Übermensch* may point to yet another meaning of 'more (*mehr*)' (BGE 230) that is not a 'more' than nature, which may allow us to reconcile Binswanger with Freud.[36] The prefix 'over' in 'overhuman' and in 'overcoming' denotes the human being's self-overcoming.[37] It does not refer to a vertical relationship that establishes a hierarchy of the human ruling 'over' the animal, as in *Beyond Good and Evil* 230, where 'more' names the human being's 'higher' or 'different' origin that transcends nature, as in the 'siren songs of the old metaphysical bird catchers who have been piping at him [the human being] all too long: "you are more, you are higher, you are of a different origin!"' (BGE 230). Rather, 'over' refers to a horizontal relationship between the human (*homo*) and the natural (*natura*). In the Nietzschean term 'overhuman', the prefix 'over' is hence used neither to separate the human from nature nor to set one above the other (Lemm 2009: 19–23). The 'over' in 'overhuman' is to remind us that it is nature that is 'more' than the human being. The reconstruction of human nature is thus not a 'return to nature' but an elevation of the human being through the recovery of the 'more' of nature, of nature's generative and creative force. The renaturalisation of the human being thus designates a movement that takes the human being 'up into a high, free, even frightful nature and naturalness' (TI 'Skirmishes' 48).[38]

Notes

1 Leiter (2013); Emden (2014); Richardson (2009).
2 On the history of historicism, see Meinecke (1972).
3 For a comparative reading of Herder and Nietzsche on history, nature and anthropology, see Bertino (2011b).
4 All translations of Binswanger are mine.
5 Nietzsche and Freud distance themselves from both the humanism and the scientism of the Enlightenment. Nietzsche, in particular, is well aware of the dialectic of Enlightenment and rejects its desire for knowledge at any price, for 'objective' truth. He invokes the Greeks, who 'knew how to live: what is needed for that is to stop bravely at the surface, the fold, the skin' (GS Preface: 4). On Nietzsche's critique of the dialectic of Enlightenment, see Adorno and Horkheimer (2002: 44); Maurer (1990).
6 Sommer (2016: 650–1); Brusotti (2014: 129).
7 I agree with Andrea Christian Bertino that 'humanization (*Vermenschlichung*)' needs to be distinguished from the more general thesis of the anthropomorphism of human knowledge in Nietzsche (that is, the idea that humans project themselves onto the world). While humanisation reflects a form of domination over the animality of the human being, anthropomorphism cannot be done away with and is a constitutive feature of perspectivism in Nietzsche (Bertino 2011a).
8 In line with my argument in Chapter 1, the problem with Leiter's account of Nietzsche's naturalism is that it does not sufficiently distinguish between these two approaches and tends to reduce the reconstruction of the human being to the deconstruction of the human being.
9 Granier (1977, 1981).
10 On the context of Binswanger's solemn homage and Freud's reaction to it, see Gasser (1997: chapter 17).
11 In HH I 106, during his so-called scientific period, Nietzsche seems to have entertained a similar fantasy: 'By the waterfall. – At the sight of a waterfall we think we see in the countless curving, twisting and breakings of the waves capriciousness and freedom of the will; but everything here is necessary, every motion mathematically calculable. So it is too in the

case of human actions; if one were all-knowing, one would be able to calculate every individual action, likewise every advance in knowledge, every error, every piece of wickedness . . . the assumption of the free-will, is itself part of the mechanism it would have to compute.' On the relation between necessity and creativity in Nietzsche, see Duncan Large (1990), who argues that the above citation is an example of Nietzsche's homage to the Enlightenment deity, his flirtation with an all-knowing, calculating intelligence. Large maintains that this mechanistic universe is an example of Nietzsche's middle period, which will be long forgotten by the time of *The Gay Science* (which contains some of Nietzsche's most scathing attacks on the prejudices of sciences) (GS 373) (Large 1990: 50, 52).

12   Leiter's naturalistic account of Nietzsche's fatalism illustrates this kind of nihilism insofar as it draws a deterministic worldview where human freedom and creativity are reduced to mere illusions (Knobe and Leiter 2007: 89–90). For Binswanger, the misunderstanding of scientific reduction in Freud is based on the erroneous translation of the 'a priori or essential possibilities of human existence into processes of genetic development (*apriorische oder wesensmässige Möglichkeiten des menschlichen Existierens in genetische Entwicklungsprozesse)*'. Such a translation of existence into natural history is for example reflected in attempts to explain 'the religious way of existing as a result of the fear and helplessness of the child [. . .] the artistic way of existing as a result of the pleasure in beautiful appearance, etc.' (Binswanger 1947: 185). Leiter's reversal of the dependence-relation between art and nature may reflect such a misconception when he holds that 'nature is not to be construed artistically; rather the work of art is to be understood naturalistically (as a product of the "basic instincts of power, nature")' (Leiter 1992: 284).

13   On the change of meaning from 'terrible' to 'eternal' in BGE 230, see Laurence Lampert (2001: 229–30). Lampert argues that this transformation reflects the mastery of the seekers of knowledge over the moral misinterpretations of human nature by tracing human nature back to its pre-moral text.

14   'The human being, a manifold, mendacious, artificial and opaque animal, uncanny to the other animal less because of his strength than because of his cunning and shrewdness' (BGE 291). This is an ongoing theme in Nietzsche's philosophy, beginning with *On Truth and Lies in an Extramoral Sense*, where he argues that the human intellect is not the sign of the human being's privileged access to knowledge but a master in the dissimulation and fabrication of illusions for the sake of self-preservation.

The human being, more than any other animal, stands in need of protection, which explains why it had to form societies to protect itself against a threatening and essentially dangerous environment (TL and GM).

15 Bertino (2011a) makes a similar point by distinguishing 'naturalization (*Vernatürlichung*)' of the human being from naturalistic reductionism.

16 In the preface of *The Antichrist*, Nietzsche acknowledges that he is speaking to posthumous readers: 'This book belongs to the very few. Perhaps none of them is even living yet' (A Preface). His readers would have to be those who have overcome humanity: 'One must be superior to human kind in force, in loftiness of soul, – in contempt . . .' (A Preface). The perspective of *The Antichrist* 14 reflects this 'misanthropism', a perspective typically associated with the scientific deconstruction of the cultural constructs of human civilisation, as Binswanger notes.

17 *The Gay Science* 115 exemplifies this idea: when one has subtracted the errors that constitute the vain beliefs in the superiority of the human being, then one has subtracted also all its so-called 'humanity': 'The four errors. – The human being has been educated by its errors: first, it saw itself only incompletely; secondly, it endowed itself with fictitious attributes; thirdly, it placed itself in a false rank order in relation to animals and nature; fourthly, it invented ever new tables of goods and for a time took them to be eternal and unconditioned, so that now this and that human drive and condition occupied first place and was ennobled as a result of this valuation. If one discounts the effect of these four errors, one has also discounted humanity, humanness and "human dignity"'.

18 Kofman (1979: 198–224).

19 Nietzsche uses the term 'stupidity' as a reference to animality. Often this is to reverse the prejudice of the human being's 'superiority' in comparison to the animals, as for example in HL 1 but also BGE 231, as I argue in Chapter 4.

20 This is also the view of Michael Allen Gillespie (1999), who argues that the psychological ground for Nietzsche's anthropology is laid out by Zarathustra in Part I of *Thus Spoke Zarathustra*, where he defines the essence of the human being as the body (rather than the soul or the self-conscious ego) and the body as nothing but affect or passion. Since passion is not a unity but a multiplicity, and each of these individual passions constantly struggles for expression, Gillespie concludes that the human being in Nietzsche is 'thus fundamentally conflictual, for the body is constantly at war with itself' (Gillespie 1999: 147). Gillespie continues that Nietzsche understands morality and religion as a response to the suffering of the human being

from the dissonances between conflicting passions by establishing peace among the passions or by devaluating this world of passions in favour of another world (ibid.). Gillespie provides a political reading of Nietzsche's insights into the psychology of conflicting passions, and argues that when Nietzsche calls for an affirmation of struggle and conflict as a means to overcoming the nihilism of morality and religion, the 'real choice is thus not between passive nihilism and a revolutionary transformation of European culture, but between a liberal bourgeois democracy and revolutionary tyranny' (ibid.: 154). According to Gillespie, Nietzsche's preference for the latter is a direct consequence of his philosophical anthropology and alerts readers of Nietzsche not to overlook the 'darker side' of his conception of human nature (ibid.). I have provided a biopolitical reading of these two aspects – the thanatopolical and the affirmative reading – of Nietzsche's thinking about the body (Lemm 2016a). See also Esposito (2008).

21 On Nietzsche taking a position against the idea of 'return to nature' in Rousseau, see TI 'Skirmishes' 48 as well as his critique of romanticism (GS 59).

22 In another posthumously published note, Nietzsche also claims that it is through the body that 'we' make value judgements: 'the body is the best advisor, the body (*Leib*) can at least be studied', something which is not true of the 'soul' (KSA 11:25[485]). See also Z, 'On the Despisers of the Body': 'But he awakened and knowing says: body (*Leib*) am I and nothing else; and soul is only a word for something about the body (*Leibe*)'.

23 On the importance of imagination in the reconstruction of the history of human transformation in Nietzsche and Aby Warburg, see also Santini (2020).

24 The question of Nietzsche's anthropology and his thinking about the body is a topic of ongoing controversy. According to Markus Meckel (1980), Nietzsche's anthropology is articulated in *Thus Spoke Zarathustra* with Zarathustra's journey as a reflection of the becoming human of the human being. According to Meckel, the central thesis of Nietzsche's anthropology is that the human being is a creator and as such continuously involved in the task of creating himself as well as creating beyond himself: 'In this creation of himself beyond himself (*Sich-über-sich-hinaus-Schaffen*), the human being is a crossing over (*Übergang*) and a going-under (*Untergang*), the one who becomes is on the way (*der Werdende auf dem Weg Seiende*) – a homo semper maior' (Meckel 1980: 179). Meckel argues that, as such, creation in the human being is distinct from divine creation in monotheistic religions. Although Meckel acknowledges that Nietzsche

thought the dimension of the creating and living body (*schaffende Leib*) (ibid.: 180), the latter is not central to his thinking about the whole nature of the human being (ibid.: 180, 208). For Meckel, what defines the human being is its capacity for creation, knowledge and love through which it continuously exceeds itself and goes beyond itself. But on the journey of becoming who they are, human beings will need to enter into communication with other human beings: 'Only insofar as the human being is spirit and not just an unmediated (*unmittelbares*) creature of nature (*Naturwesen*), can the human being be meaningfully conceived as a being that goes beyond itself, communicates and mediates. The human being must first be educated to be a human being. Only when the human being goes beyond itself does it realize its humanness and this requires a process of communication between human beings' (ibid.: 208). Meckel finds this idea exemplified by Zarathustra's journey and his exchange with the higher human beings. Zarathustra's journey reflects the paradox between, on the one hand, the task to create and communicate a new idea of the human being, and, on the other hand, the task to lead the human back to its unmediated naturalness. This paradox is reflected in Nietzsche's conception of thought as a function of organic life. Nietzsche wants to reinscribe the human being back into nature to the extent that thought only insofar as it is embodied remains unmediated and thus overcomes the division between nature and the human being. But, according to Meckel, and this is where I disagree with him, the thinking body is not self-reflective. Meckel concludes that since creativity, knowledge and love in the human being defined as a being that goes beyond itself rest on the human being's capacity to reflect on itself and on its actions, Nietzsche posits reason as that which constitutes human nature: 'as such Nietzsche also considers reason to be the constitutive feature of the human being' (ibid.: 208). Here the question is, what does Nietzsche mean by reason? Volker Gerhardt (2009) reaches a different conclusion in his essay 'The Body, the Self and the Ego', arguing that Nietzsche's talk of the 'great reason' of the body and 'small reason' of consciousness makes sense only by way of an aesthetic interpretation. According to Gerhardt, the body is, on the one hand, 'dependent upon, and determined by, the natural and historical condition it comes from and by which it remains necessarily bound. On the other hand, the body determines *solely by itself* the beginning and the end of the sense and senses at its disposal: through the particular configuration of its organization the body determines the rhythm and the time of the activity it pursues. [. . .] Thus it is in fact the body which provides the order in which the sense of a living existence is attained' (Gerhardt 2009: 285). This is also the view of Patrick Wotling (2008), for whom the body reflects primarily a complex ordering (hierarchy) of multiple conflicting and contradictory drives according to relationships of command and obedience, an idea also discussed at length in Wolfgang Müller-Lauter (1999), the organism as struggle. As such, the body is cohesion, the facilitator of collaboration and communication that affirms a certain 'community of nature' (KSA 11:34[123]; Wotling 2008: 159). Wotling argues that the 'body is language' (Wotling 2008: 159) and the body is the activity of interpretation (ibid.: 165). Wotling finds this idea of community expressed in Nietzsche's claim that 'our body is in fact nothing but a social structure composed of multiple souls' (BGE 19). By reintroducing the multiple souls within the body, Nietzsche points to the fact it is impossible to separate physiology from psychology, theory from practice, or in other words that insight into physiology remains subject to interpretation, an idea that may have been inspired by Wilhelm Roux. On the crossing of physiology and psychology in Nietzsche, see also Wotling (1995). Here Wotling's reading of the body and its creation of orders complements Gerhardt's point: 'The sort of sense which is intelligible requires a specific organ, and for Nietzsche – as for Plato, Kant or Hegel – this organ is the faculty of reason' (Gerhardt 2009: 288). However, this idea of sense and reason presupposes a conception of the body as a unity or a whole that expresses '*the whole of the body*' (ibid.). Gerhardt claims that 'reason is that which makes itself manifest in the expressions of the body – just as the beautiful does in art' (ibid.: 289). In this account, Gerhardt's reading of reason as an organ of the living body rather than as a faculty that transcends it provides a convincing argument against Meckel's conception of reason and communication in Nietzsche's anthropology.

25   See Granier (1981: 101).

26   See in comparison BGE 226 on the sense of duty in Nietzsche's free spirits in the chapter on 'Our Virtues'.

27   On the question of the overcoming of the human, see also Gerard Visser's (1999) position on Nietzsche's *Übermensch*. Visser argues that in Nietzsche the overcoming of the human being means the end of the concept 'human being' and the beginning of a new concept '*Übermensch*'. The latter can no longer be understood as a general definition of the nature or essence of the human being but rather depicts that which is singular and irreducible in each and every human being: 'The *Übermensch* is no longer a human being but an individual' (Visser 1999: 107). For Visser, Nietzsche's question is

'whether every individual should not rather be an experiment to achieve a higher species (*Gattung*) than the human being by virtue of their most individual things' (KSA 9:6[158]).

28 Christa Davis Acampora (2006) coins the term 'artful naturalism' to capture this aspect of Nietzsche's naturalism.

29 According to Paul Bishop (2009), the naturalisation of humanity is also at stake in Carl Gustav Jung's psychology. From his perspective, by calling for a new conception of nature, one that dismisses the notion of laws in nature, Nietzsche calls for a new conception of the human being (HH 3).

30 On the controversies around Freud's relationship to Nietzsche, see Gasser (1997) and Assoun (2000). See also Tinneke Beekman (2009/2010) for a very useful overview of Freud's main objections against philosophy (including Nietzsche's philosophy). Beekman shows that 'Freud hasn't brought in an element against philosophy that Nietzsche wouldn't have understood' and that therefore 'Nietzsche cannot be the object of Freud's contempt for philosophers' (Beekman 2009/2010: 114). Instead, Beekman argues that 'Nietzsche, the great psychologist', already anticipated the limits to which Freud admits to and that therefore Freud's 'meta-psychology' would not be any less metaphysical than he claims Nietzsche's philosophy to be (ibid.: 117).

31 See Alan D. Schrift, who argues that the *Übermensch* is Nietzsche's answer to Kant's questions: 'what is the human being' (Schrift 2001: 48, 47–62).

32 Granier seems to think that Freud also adopted the term *homo natura* from Nietzsche but as far as I am aware it is Binswanger who applies Nietzsche's coinage to describe Freud's conception of the human being. According to Gasser, Freud was not aware that Binswanger was actually citing Nietzsche when he defined his conception of the human being in terms of *homo natura*.

33 Karl Löwith (1933) makes a similar point in relation to Nietzsche: that Nietzsche's reconstruction of human nature is largely inspired by the historical-philosophical examples of natural humanity provided by Greek antiquity and the human being in the Renaissance, as well as a few individual examples from modernity such as Goethe and Napoleon.

34 On the Greek influences of Nietzsche's conception of nature, see Strong (2015); Hatab (2015).

35 See also Nietzsche on this point: 'The renaturalization of the human being requires the willingness to accept the sudden and unpredictable (*Durchkreuzende*)' (KSA 9:11[228]).

36 Recall aphorism 230 in *Beyond Good and Evil*: 'To translate the human
being back to nature; to become master over the many vain and overly
enthusiastic interpretations and connotations that have so far been
scrawled and painted over that eternal basic text *homo natura*; to see to it
that the human being henceforth stands before the human being as even
today, hardened in the discipline of science, he stands before the rest of
nature, with intrepid Oedipus eyes and sealed Odysseus ears, deaf to the
siren songs of old metaphysical bird catchers who have been piping at him
all too long: "you are more, you are higher, you are of different origin!"'
(BGE 230).

37 On this point, see Ansell-Pearson (2000).

38 See also 'The renaturalization of the human being in the nineteenth
century (the eighteenth century is the century of elegance, finesse and
generous sentiments). Not "return to nature": for their never existed
a human naturalness (*natürliche Menschheit*). Scholastics un- and anti-
natural values is the rule, is the beginning; the human being reaches
nature only after a long struggle – it never "returns" to it . . . Nature,
i.e., to dare to be immoral like nature' (KSA 21:10[53].182).

4

Biopolitics, Sexuality, and Social Transformation

Friedrich Nietzsche's pronouncements on the 'Eternal-Feminine', on 'woman as such' and on the necessary antagonism between men and women have earned him a reputation as a misogynist and a reactionary with respect to women's claims to be recognised as legal and political equals. Perhaps none of Nietzsche's reflections in this area is more infamous than the exchange between Zarathustra and 'the little old woman' who counsels the prophet of the overman: 'Are you visiting woman? Do not forget the whip' (Z I: 'Of Old and Young Women'). And yet, there is also widespread agreement that Nietzsche's insights on the relation between sexuality and morality have been instrumental in articulating great, indeed emancipatory, revisions of our understanding of how sexuality functions in making us who we are, from Sigmund Freud to Michel Foucault and Judith Butler. One of the reasons why such contrary views on the subject of Nietzsche and sexuality emerge is due to his discourse on human nature. The recourse to *homo natura* may lend itself to be interpreted as a naturalisation of sexuality and run afoul the feminist belief that biology is not destiny. But as I have argued so far, this is to miss Nietzsche's main thesis, according to which the recovery of nature is the ground of transformation.

In this chapter I offer the hypothesis that Nietzsche envisages the naturalisation of the human being, 'retranslating the human back into nature' (BGE 230), as a liberating because empowering experience that allows individuals to rediscover in their sexuality a creative and transformative force. As argued in previous chapters, *homo natura* is an expression that Nietzsche employs in order to de-essentialise the human being. Therefore, the discourse on sexuality found in Nietzsche does not identify sex as the essential core of truth in the human being. Indeed, only by adopting a Nietzschean analysis of the 'will to truth' as a will to power could Foucault famously identify the dominating role of *scientia sexualis* in late modernity (Foucault 1990b). Everything in Nietzsche argues against his having had recourse to metaphysical ideas of truth and of being precisely when thinking about sexuality. That is why it makes sense for Butler to say that 'for our purposes, this Nietzschean criticism [of the metaphysics of substance] becomes instructive when it is applied to the psychological categories that govern much popular and theoretical thinking about gender identity' (Butler 1999: 28). Likewise, as Jacques Derrida (1998) has argued in his interpretations of Nietzsche's discourse on woman and truth, Nietzsche interprets the phenomenon of sexuality – as it ranges from its biological (sex) to its social (gender) articulations – to denote the otherness, alterity or *différance* of (human) nature. This otherness of human nature allows individuals and even social relations to withdraw from discourses of truth, whether scientific, moral or metaphysical, that reflect forms of power over nature.[1] According to Nietzsche, the anti-moral virtue of probity that enjoins a critique of the will to truth does not articulate this critique as a discourse about or of sexuality, but requires that the individual understand itself as a sexual being.

Probity, not the will to truth, shows that 'the degree and kind of a human being's sexuality (*Grad und Art der Geschlechtlichkeit*) reach up to the ultimate pinnacle of its spirit' (BGE 75).[2]

As discussed in Chapter 3, Jean Granier's reading of *homo natura* in Nietzsche and Freud showed that their fundamental point of agreement is the idea that human nature is inaccessible and withdraws from every attempt to construct the human being as a pure object of knowledge. Philosophers with a commitment to probity acknowledge that the discovery of the 'basic text' *homo natura* always only proceeds through mythologies and imaginaries that create and recreate nature at the same time that they discover it. Also, Ludwig Binswanger's interpretation of *homo natura* in Nietzsche and Freud identifies their fundamental difference in the absence of a theory of human transformation in Freud, one that Binswanger, by contrast, finds exemplified in Nietzsche's conception of the overhuman. In this chapter, I argue that Nietzsche's conception of sexuality offers yet another argument in favour of a transformational account of human nature.

For Nietzsche, the question of the future of the human being is imminently contingent on whether the human being can re-embody sexuality and affirm itself as a 'more natural' sexual being. Sexual nature as Nietzsche conceives of it is not a biological given that predetermines the functioning of our bodies. Rather, the realisation of sexuality embodies the task of 'becoming who we are' by returning to nature as chaos of drives. This perhaps makes possible the claim that for Nietzsche – as for some of his psychoanalytically informed interpreters like Luce Irigaray – sexual difference is anterior to any social or symbolic construction, but not in the sense that 'sex' (in some aspect) is somehow a 'natural' given (as opposed to a 'cultural' construction) (Irigaray

1991). Rather, it is in the sense that the Dionysian 'real' occupies a poetic-mythological anteriority with respect to the Apollonian structures of the symbolic, and it is only in relation to this anteriority that a creative-sexual life can be established. Thus, the 'reactionary' air of Nietzsche's critique of modern feminism is in great part due to his attempt to recover an archaic, long-forgotten understanding or experience of nature, not for its own sake but as an occasion for a forward movement that opens the future and is geared towards the metamorphosis and transformation of the human being. Nietzsche's thinking about human nature is concerned with the question of who else we could become and thus prepares a cultural renewal of humanity.

Butler argues that:

> the internal coherence or unity of either gender, man or woman, thereby requires both a stable and oppositional heterosexuality. [. . .] The institution of a compulsory and naturalized heterosexuality requires and regulates gender as a binary relation in which the masculine term is differentiated from a feminine term, and this differentiation is accomplished through the practice of heterosexual desire. (Butler 1999: 30–1)

I show that Nietzsche's critique of modern feminism, coupled with his anti-modern recovery of an archaic, Dionysian approach to sexual difference, are functional to an intention to disrupt this normative heterosexuality. At the same time, I hope to show that this 'backward-looking' strategy in Nietzsche does not fall into the fallacy of presupposing a 'utopian notion of a sexuality freed from heterosexual constructs, a sexuality beyond "sex"' (ibid.: 39). Nor does his discourse on the destiny that is singularity amount to a 'return to biology as the ground of a specific feminine sexuality or meaning' (ibid.). However, it is an interesting question whether

Nietzsche's discourse on sexuality is closer in spirit to Butler's own proposal based on the performative deconstruction of gender, such that 'the repetition of heterosexual constructs within sexual cultures both gay and straight may well be the inevitable site of the denaturalization and mobiliziation of gender categories' (ibid.: 41), or whether it is closer to Gayle Rubin's 'revolution in kinship' that would 'eradicate' the 'exchange of women, the traces of which are evident not only in the contemporary institutionalization of heterosexuality, but in the residual psychic norms (the institutionalization of the psyche) which sanction and construct sexuality and gender identity in heterosexual terms' (ibid.: 95).[3] The answer to this question would be simpler if we knew who was meant to receive the famous whip and for which use it was intended.[4]

In the *History of Sexuality: Volume 1*, Foucault points out how strange it is, given the prevalent Freudian 'repressive hypothesis', that sexuality had been so much and so openly discussed in the Victorian age, to which Nietzsche also belonged. In reality, for Foucault this proliferation of sexual discourse betrays the fact that sex had been figured as the new truth of the subject, and this truth had to be confessed to if the subject could be said to know itself. For Foucault psychoanalysis belongs, at the margins, to this tradition, perhaps as that form of confession that would elicit the liberating awareness that there was nothing, no sin, to confess after all. Sexualisation was thus the main form that the will to truth adopted in order to constitute individuals as subjects.

In the subsequent volumes of the *History of Sexuality*, Foucault traces the archaeology of this confessional approach to truth back through early Christian pastoral practices to Greco-Roman forms of self-examination, all of which drew ultimately from Socratic grounds. Only in his last Lectures at the Collège de France did

Foucault work out an alternative or counter-concept to the idea of confession, namely, the concept of *parrhesia*, or speaking truth to power. As I have indicated already, for Foucault the most radical form of *parrhesia* was practiced by the Cynics. However, Foucault does not pursue systematically the inverse path from Cynic *parrhesia* back to sexuality, except in his non-academic interventions into the sexual politics of his day and, in particular, with the theorisation of what today may be called queer 'forms of life' (Foucault 1997: 135–40). In what follows, I attempt to argue that, had Foucault retraced his steps back to the Victorian age, he might have recognised in Nietzsche a particularly Cynic approach to sexuality. Thus, my approximation in this chapter to Nietzsche's discourse on women, men and sexuality will be focused on the relation between probity or *Redlichkeit* (Nietzsche's term for *parrhesia*) and the discourse of sexuality.

Only towards the end of the first volume of the *History of Sexuality* does Foucault reveal the reason why the dispositive of sexuality emerges: the reason was due to biopolitics, namely, to a transformation of power that saw biological life as its most proper object. Since sex had been confirmed, in the biological thinking of the nineteenth century, as the wellspring of life, and social reproduction meant first and foremost the reproduction of the species, it was evident that sexuality, by being at the crossroads of nature and society, would become the decisive instrument of modern biopolitics (Foucault 1990b). Nietzsche's discourse on sexuality needs to be situated within the broader biopolitical context of the nineteenth century with the simultaneous discovery of the sexuality of nature and the sociality of sexuality. As Wolfgang Riedel shows, the discovery of the hetero/dual-sexuality (*Zwiegeschlechtlichkeit*) of life lies at the centre of the biological concept of nature in the nineteenth century: 'Around

1900, whoever wants to talk about nature – whether in biology, philosophy or literature – must speak of sexuality' (Riedel 1996: xiii). On this view, the sexualisation of nature is a distinct feature of philosophical and literary anthropology at this time, and thus it is also reflected, adopted and adapted in Nietzsche's discourse on *homo natura*. Likewise, another distinguishing feature of the nineteenth-century discourse on sexuality is the emergence of theories of society that are based on the sexual division of labour (Rogers 1978). According to Andreas Urs Sommer, Nietzsche was aware of those contemporary political thinkers that identified the sexual drive as the foundation of society (Sommer 2016: 656).[5] In this chapter, I argue that Nietzsche takes up and responds to both the sexualisation of nature and the socialisation of sexuality in a consciously biopolitical way in his thinking about the ancient Greeks and, in particular, in his discovery of the Dionysian. Roberto Esposito offers an interesting hypothesis of how Nietzsche's focus on the Dionysian fits in with the biopolitical situation of which sexuality, per Foucault's hypothesis, plays a crucial role. For Esposito, Nietzsche criticises the incipient liberalism of the nineteenth century – and in the case of sexuality, this critique takes aim at the demand for equal rights between men and women – because he understands them as a function of heightening 'immunity' or 'securitizing' individuals against the social or common bond itself. On this hypothesis, Nietzsche's turn to will to power and to the Dionysian is a paradoxical moment of 'hyperimmunity' in which society is called to protect itself against too much protection (at the individual level). This leads to Nietzsche's radicalisation of biopolitics in a sexist and racist way, according to which 'life' can be heightened only through a process of 'selection' between higher and lower forms of life, that is, only by doing away with those egalitarian and liberal legal and political barriers that protect every individual's life in the same way (Esposito 2008, 2011). In what follows, I suggest an alternative, more affirmative reading of Nietzsche's biopolitics in relation to his discourse on sexuality and the Dionysian, again exemplified by the Cynic form of life.

Homo natura and Feminism

The series of aphorisms 231–9 in *Beyond Good and Evil* immediately following Nietzsche's reference to *homo natura* contain his famously controversial claims on 'woman as such' and the 'basic problem "man and woman"'. These texts are typically set aside as a different subject or unrelated topic that is only contingently related to his thinking about human nature and the task of renaturalisation.[6] In contrast to existing readings of *Beyond Good and Evil*, I argue that Nietzsche's pursuit of the theme of *homo natura* does not end with aphorism 230. Rather, aphorisms *Beyond Good and Evil* 231–9 introduce sexuality as a third element in the relationship between the human being (*homo*) and nature (*natura*) that is crucial to the transformation of human civilisation towards a more genuine and natural humanity. This cultural–political dimension of Nietzsche's thinking about human nature has so far not received sufficient attention by scholars, who have either been overly concerned with the question of scientific naturalism in Nietzsche's philosophy or with accusing and defending him from charges of misogyny.[7]

In order to understand how *homo natura* (BGE 230) relates to the problem field of sexuality (BGE 231–9), we need to take a closer look at aphorism 231. *Beyond Good and Evil* 231 functions both as a bridge from the question of *homo natura* to

118

the question of sexuality and as a transition from discussing the nature of the human being to treating the nature of the individual.[8] In BGE 231, Nietzsche introduces the idea of a 'granite of spiritual *fatum*', something unchangeable and untransformable, 'deep down (*da unten*)', that inherently defines the nature and destiny of each and every individual. This reference to the 'granite of spiritual *fatum*' is often associated by interpreters with some aspect of sex or sexuality that is somehow anterior to any social or symbolic construction of gender. In feminist interpretations of Nietzsche, this text among others has led to a debate on the question of whether Nietzsche is an essentialist or anti-essentialist about human nature and sexuality.

In her thorough treatment of *Nietzsche's Women*, Carol Diethe advances a comparison between Jean-Jacques Rousseau's and Nietzsche's portrayals of 'female sexuality as manipulative':

> Admittedly, there is a big distinction between Rousseau's version of woman's nature, where the ideal woman is constructed as 'man's better self' and stands as prototype for Goethe's Eternal-Womanly, and Nietzsche's notion of the predatory woman propelled by the 'will to pregnancy'. Both men, however, start from the premise that there is a separate female 'nature' which can be analysed without recourse to social factors. (Diethe 1996: 67)[9]

Diethe acknowledges that Nietzsche broke with Wilhelmine society's 'denial of the respectable woman's sexuality' by declaring that 'women should and did enjoy the sex act as much as men' (ibid.: 47). She also sees that some of Nietzsche's most overtly misogynist remarks refer to 'society' women competing in the 'marriage mart', as evidenced by *Beyond Good and Evil* 237 (ibid.: 68).[10] However, she claims this 'other Nietzsche, the man who sees women unfairly treated and intercedes on their behalf' is overshadowed by Nietzsche's adherence to Arthur Schopenhauer's 'view of sexual intercourse as a manifestation of the *Wille zum Leben* (will to life)' that ends up being determinant for his views on 'woman's sexuality as inextricably and ineluctably bound up with child-rearing' (ibid.: 47). Again, her point is that 'Nietzsche's determined refusal to take any account of social factors which took the gender debate "beyond the whip" makes any discussion of woman's inherently different nature (a concept which this author strongly refutes in any case) lop-sided from the outset' (ibid.: 71).[11] Diethe assumes, without question, that 'female sexuality' is tied up in Nietzsche with an unchangeable conception of human nature that is impervious to social transformation.

Other scholars analysing Nietzsche through a feminist lens, though, see in Nietzsche's critique of the 'woman question' of his times a decidedly anti-essentialist bend. Lynne Tirrell, for example, argues that: 'it is clear that Nietzsche did not take sexual dualism to be an unalterable fact about the world' (Tirrell 1998: 206). She interprets Nietzsche's prediction that 'in the three or four civilised countries in Europe women can through a few centuries of education be made into anything, even men: not in the sexual sense (*geschlechtlichen Sinne*), to be sure, but in every other sense' (HH 425) as a sign of his anti-essentialism, since from the perspective of essentialism such a transformation of gender would be impossible (Tirrell 1998: 206).[12] What Tirrell finds lacking in Nietzsche, though, is 'the complexities of the power issues associated with sexual dualism that defines the category "woman"' (ibid.: 207). Similarly, against the standard readings of Nietzsche as 'an essentialist, an opponent of women's rights, an enthusiast of masculine virtue, and an advocate of male domination' (Higgins 1998: 131), Kathleen Marie Higgins argues that '*The Gay Science* presents an entrée into gender theory that is genuinely exciting' (ibid.: 138). She acknowledges that whilst Nietzsche may be a 'biological foundationalist, he is not a biological determinist' (ibid.: 144): 'Even if he is still locked into the notion of a heterosexual binarism (a matter that itself is debatable), his suggestions that there are many types of women with different psychological takes on reality initiate an exploration of the possibilities' (ibid.: 146).

Whether they agree or disagree with the possibility of changes to gender being brought about by social practices in Nietzsche's theory, feminist interpreters share a common assumption that his discourses on sexual difference are tied to an invariance of nature. The problem lies with the belief that Nietzsche clearly distinguishes between sex and gender, that is, between 'the biological potential to play one role rather than another in reproduction' and 'the contingently assigned roles that a society attaches to those who are biologically male or female' (ibid.: 131).[13] The distinction may help to show that 'Nietzsche . . . urged his readers to recognize the contingency of gender roles and to consider the desirability of changing them' (ibid.).

But in maintaining a standard distinction between sexuality (fixed) and gender (constructed), this kind of interpretation does not pose a problem for the kind of reading of *Beyond Good and Evil* proposed by Laurence Lampert, who argues that the 'granite of spiritual *fatum*' is a reference to the 'sex' of the individual, the 'fact' that one is born either male or female and that this dualism in the nature of the individual is subordinate to the higher logic of the preservation of human species life through sexuated reproduction (Lampert 2001: 233–42). Under the banner of 'sexuality', this view advances an essentialist conception of nature with sexuality as that feature of human life that cannot be formed and transformed. From this perspective, sexuality is what *prevents* the individual from radically altering itself. By contrast, my point in this chapter is precisely to question this assumption found in feminist readings of Nietzsche according to which sexuality and/or sexual difference, in contra-position to gender, escapes or blocks social transformation. Rather, recourse to the anti-essentialism of *homo natura* and its relation to sexuality and/or sexual difference prepares the ground for the transformation of sexuality and gender. On my view, Nietzsche's conception of nature is transformational, and sexuality plays a crucial role in the renaturalisation of the human being and its transformation towards a more natural humanity.

Nietzsche's thinking about human nature stands at the centre of Chapter 7, 'Our Virtues', of *Beyond Good and Evil*. This is the very same chapter in which Diethe thinks that Nietzsche 'defends the position of woman as feather-brained dependent' (Diethe 1996: 45). In this chapter, Nietzsche sets the tone for a cultural renewal of Europe that would counteract the process of liberal Enlightenment underway by raising the question of what virtues, if any, are required to realise a transition (*Übergang*) towards a morality beyond good and evil (van Tongeren 2014: 148). In 'Our Virtues', Nietzsche suggests that the renaturalisation (*Vernatürlichung*) of the human being is the first step towards such a cultural renewal. Furthermore, renaturalisation is a task that requires probity. However, renaturalisation as Nietzsche understands it entails that virtue – 'supposing probity is our virtue (*Redlichkeit, gesetzt das dies unsere Tugend ist*)' (BGE 227) – could no longer be conceived of as moral virtue. Probity as a moral virtue is overcome in the transition towards a morality beyond good and evil. As such, the transformation of virtue and of the human being is both a going under

(*Untergang*) and a going over (*Übergang*) from the moral to the extra-moral.[14]

The question Nietzsche thematises is the role played by 'woman as such' and the 'basic problem of "man and woman"' both in the Enlightenment project and in his counter-proposal. The idea of anti-moral probity is worked out by Nietzsche in the question of the relation of woman and truth, and turns on the question of sexuality as 'spiritual *fatum*'.[15] Given the prominent role probity plays in the chapter 'Our Virtues', commentators have argued that sections 231–9 of *Beyond Good and Evil* exemplify how Nietzsche conceives of probity beyond good and evil, with his personal views on woman and on the warfare between the sexes serving as a demonstration of probity in practice.[16] According to Christa D. Acampora and Keith Ansell-Pearson (2011), aphorisms 231–9 of *Beyond Good and Evil* show Nietzsche exposing himself, his stupidity (*Dummheit*), 'as a necessary aspect of the philosopher's commitment to honesty and seeing things for what they nakedly are: assumptions, presuppositions, prejudice – often dressed up as eternal veritas and pearls of wisdom' (Acampora and Ansell-Pearson 2011: 168). Acampora and Ansell-Pearson take the sections to demonstrate how Nietzsche thinks free spirits practice their honesty, that is, 'the key virtue that he is trying to illustrate in the denouement to part VII of Nietzsche's book' (ibid.: 169). This view culminates in Maudemarie Clarke's (1998) position, according to which aphorisms 231–9 are more about Nietzsche's truth ('*meine* Wahrheiten'), his stupidities about sexuality, and less about 'woman as such' (BGE 231).

While I agree with commentators that the voice of BGE 231–9 is that of the philosopher in pursuit of truth, that is, the thinker committed to probity (*redliche Denker*) who has rediscovered the 'basic text' of *homo natura*, I disagree with the view that Nietzsche's stupidities (*Dummheiten*), his truths (*meine Wahrheiten*) about 'woman as such', are unrelated to his thinking about sexuality and its function in overcoming morality. As if the theme of 'woman as such' and of sexuality could have been replaced by any other theme to illustrate probity as a transformative virtue that leads humanity beyond good and evil. As if for Nietzsche to be '*redlich*' would require nothing but admitting that one's truths about women are 'stupid'. By contrast, I argue that the overcoming of probity as a moral virtue requires an affirmation of sexuality as a force of nature that enables human self-overcoming and transformation. Sexuality provides the key to Nietzsche's thinking about probity in the chapter 'Our Virtues' of *Beyond Good and Evil*, and not the other way around.

But how does sexuality relate to (social and cultural) transformation? On my reading, Nietzsche addresses the biopolitical driver for social transformation of human nature in his discussion of the 'basic problem "man and woman"' (BGE 238). In Nietzsche's conception of the Dionysian, nature becomes the negation of reason and morality, and is linked with a conception of chaos as anarchy and irreducible plurality of drives and sexuality (Riedel 1996: 191). In recognising the human being as a living being that is continuous with nature, in denying any cardinal difference between animals and humans, Nietzsche places the task of fashioning *homo natura* under the name of Dionysus in order to identify in sexuality the primary site of the liberation of the modern individual from western, that is, primarily Christian ideas of human nature (BGE 238). But in Nietzsche, Dionysus also stands for an embracing of sexuality as a vehicle of social transformation reflected in the Homeric idea of nature as a 'war' between the sexes. It is the site of relations of power and the respective dynamics of domination and liberation.

Already for Nietzsche, the debate on the Dionysian is decidedly biopolitical: the Dionysian approach to sexuality understands it from the start as entanglement of nature and politics. As clearly seen by the early Frankfurt School, and more recently as argued by Esposito, the possibility of employing Nietzsche's critique of bourgeois Christian civilisation, even perhaps of the dimension of the Apollonian itself, on behalf of a liberated Dionysian life, for the purpose of legitimating a biopolitics-cum-thanatopolitics, was real. This point was already perceived by Alfred Baeumler in his 1928 article, 'Nietzsche und Bachofen'. Baeumler argues that Johann Jakob Bachofen's recovery of matriarchy, based on his discovery of the struggle carried forth by the Apollonian masculine deities against the Dionysian feminine divinities, sought to bring back into European consciousness a Greek approach to sexuality that would problematise its bourgeois, Christian regimentation (Baeumler 1928). Acknowledging Bachofen's influence on Nietzsche's recovery of Dionysus, Baeumler's thesis, however, is that Nietzsche ultimately rejects Bachofen's view and the priority of Dionysus on the grounds that it is not 'virile' enough and, instead, prioritises a Greek conception of martial 'heroism' centred on the category of the *agon*. As is well known, Baeumler later joined the Nazi movement and became one of its central ideologues. He was a crucial proponent of the appropriation of Nietzsche's philosophy to the Nazi war effort (Whyte 2008). By way of contrast, the interpretation I put forward here does not separate the dimension of *agon* from the Dionysian approach to sexuality, and sees in this matriarchical focus one of the keys that accounts for why sexuality in Nietzsche is central to both the renaturalisation of the human being and the transformation of social relationships by overcoming forms of domination towards higher and freer forms of sociability and political organisation. To illustrate this point, this chapter concludes on some preliminary ideas on Nietzsche's social imaginary and his vision of a future culture and society that may have been inspired by the relationship between sexuality and *parrhesia* in the ancient Cynics. In my account, the transition to a morality beyond good and evil occurs with a decoupling of the will to truth from moral ideals, in particular, the false ideals of human nature. This decoupling was first put into practice by the ancient Cynics in their relation to embodiment and sexuality as a way to overcome the barriers that society erects between nature and the human being. I suggest that Nietzsche's thinking about nature, sexuality and politics may find a precursor in the ancient Cynics.

Sexuality, Individual Nature and Self-Knowledge

The affirmation of the human being as a natural and living being, as *homo natura*, leads Nietzsche to enquire in *Beyond Good and Evil* 231 into the nature of the individual and its quest for self-knowledge and self-transformation. It is worth remembering, first, that the discovery of the 'basic text *homo natura*' does not lead Nietzsche to postulate an anthropology, a series of universal claims about human nature; and, second, that it is not the starting point for a scientific or biological reconstruction of human species life. Instead, Nietzsche takes his readers to the heart of his own quest for knowledge and self-knowledge, his own 'spiritual *fatum*':

> But at the bottom of *us* (*im Grunde von uns*), really 'deep down (*da unten*)', there is, of course, something unteachable (*Unbelehrbares*), some granite of spiritual fatum, of predetermined

decision and answer (*vorherbestimmter Entscheidung und Antwort*) to predetermined selected questions (*vorherbestimmte ausgelesene Fragen*). Whenever a cardinal problem is at stake, there speaks an unchangeable (*unwandelbares*) 'this is I'; about man and woman, for example, a thinker cannot relearn (*umlernen*) but only finish learning (*auslernen*) – only discover ultimately how this is 'settled in him (*feststeht*)'. At times, we find certain solutions of problems that inspire strong faith in us; some call them henceforth their 'convictions'. Later – we see them only as steps to self-knowledge, signposts to the problem we are – rather, to the great stupidity *we* are, to our spiritual *fatum*, to what is unteachable (*Unbelehrbaren*) very 'deep down (*da unten*)'. After this abundant civility (*Artigkeit*) that I have just evidenced in relation to myself I shall perhaps be permitted more readily to state a few truths about 'woman as such' – assuming that it is now known from the outset how very much these are after all only – *my* truths. (BGE 231)

The question of what Nietzsche is referring to 'at the bottom of *us* (*im Grunde von uns*), really "deep down (*da unten*)"', 'a granite of spiritual *fatum*' and why this granite of spiritual destiny points to 'the problem we are – rather, to the great stupidity *we* are' has puzzled many commentators.

Lampert suggests that Nietzsche's thoughts on 'woman as such' are 'the thoughts of a thinker whose cruel task is to recover the basic text *homo natura* and use that recovered text in a war against modern ideas' (Lampert 2001: 233). From here, Lampert infers that when Nietzsche speaks of the 'deep down (*da unten*)', he is speaking of maleness and femaleness as differences that are natural and unchangeable:

Contrary to modern ideas, maleness and femaleness are differences given deep down, part of the unteachable, untransformable inheritance of our animal and human past. Set at the end of 'Our

Virtues', these sections [aphorisms 231–9] argue that the modern idea of equality as it applies to male and female paints over the basic text of species inheritance. (Ibid.).

According to Lampert, the sections on 'man and woman' continue the chief issue of section 230, which discusses the two opposing wills of the spirit. This continuity seems to lend support to Lampert's view that Nietzsche is an essentialist about human nature, with sexuality not only standing as a marker of the difference between 'man and woman' but also as the ultimate drive that defines human species life.

Lampert argues that the 'basic will of the spirit' transcends gender:

> the final theme of this chapter ['Our Virtues'], the warfare between the sexes, expresses in the natural divisions of gender the two inclinations of mind, the basic will of the mind to create and sustain artful surfaces and the renegade will to penetrate to true depth. Nietzsche's position with respect to the sexes would then be ontological and epistemological in its roots; the cosmetic or female arts contrast with and are inevitably at war with the wilful penetration of surfaces by the intellect. (Ibid.: 233).[17]

In contrast to Lampert, I do not read Nietzsche's 'deep down (*da unten*)' as a reference to the 'most basic truth of sexual difference', of 'maleness and femaleness' as 'differences given deep down' (ibid.: 233, 235). Lampert falsely equates the 'granite of spiritual *fatum*' with sexual difference, as if Nietzsche's point is that each individual's spiritual destiny is nothing but a biological fact, whereas he clearly states that this destiny is a function of a 'predetermined decision and answer (*vorherbestimmter Entscheidung und Antwort*) to predetermined selected questions (*vorherbestimmte ausgelesene Fragen*)' (BGE 231).

Note that in *Beyond Good and Evil* 230, Nietzsche introduces the idea of a 'basic will of the spirit (*Grundwillen des Geistes*)' and defines it as a tension between two opposing and antagonistic drives. There is, on the one hand, the will to appropriate the foreign and make it one's own in view of growth and a feeling of increased strength; and, on the other hand, there is the will to forgetfulness, a decisive closing down of one's horizon and affirmation of ignorance (BGE 230). Nietzsche continues that the latter is best understood as a 'will to mere appearance (*Schein*), to simplification, to mask, to cloaks, in short, to the surface' and introduces the 'inclination of the seeker after knowledge (*Hang des Erkennenden*)', another word for the will to truth, as a counteracting drive that 'insists on profundity, multiplicity, and thoroughness (*die Dinge tief, vielfach, gründlich nimmt und nehmen will*), with a will which is a kind of cruelty of the intellectual conscience and taste (*Grausamkeit des intellektuellen Gewissens und Geschmacks*)' (BGE 230). In my view, Lampert misinterprets the basic will of the spirit as a tension between the two opposing and antagonistic drives, that is, as an antagonism between the drive to ignorance and the drive to knowledge. However, Nietzsche compares the basic will of the spirit to the metabolism of the stomach: torn between the drive to grow (to appropriate the other, the foreign, and to make it one's own) and the drive to protect itself against that which it cannot digest (to close down one's horizon and to preserve oneself against the other). In this regard, the basic will of the spirit has been compared to the will to power, which Nietzsche introduces in *Beyond Good and Evil* 22.

Against the backdrop of life as will to power, the will to truth, the 'inclination of the seeker of knowledge (*Erkennende*)' seems anti-natural and opposed to life. In response to this apparent contradiction, Nietzsche is keen to show that philosophy is not anti-natural and claims that at the basis of the will to truth, we find the cruelty of the animal: 'in all desire to know (*Erkennen-Wollen*) is a drop of cruelty' (BGE 229).[18] From the perspective of Nietzsche's affirmation of animality and the cultural productivity of cruelty, the discontent of human civilisation does not arise from the will to truth per se, but from a will to truth that stands under the rule of morality (and of modern ideas) insofar as the latter reflect a denial of the cultural (transformational) forces of nature and animality. As such, Nietzsche advocates for a renaturalisation of philosophy that liberates the will to truth from morality. The latter is exemplified by the probity of the thinker who confirms that at the basis of all knowledge we find the cruelty of the animal (BGE 229).

From the perspective of Nietzsche's critique of morality, aphorism 231 is in the first instance concerned with the question of what the discovery of 'the basic text *homo natura*' means for philosophy, or, in other words, what it means to philosophise beyond good and evil. Just as in aphorism 229, where Nietzsche reminds his readers of the human being's so-called animal past, the 'savage cruel beast (*wilde grausame Thier*)' (BGE 229) that stands at the beginning of culture, aphorism 231 begins by placing the human being back among animal and plant life. Aphorism 231 emphasises the continuity between nature and the human being and refers us back to the (human) body and its metabolism: 'Learning changes (*verwandelt*) us; it does what all nourishment does which also does not merely "preserve" – as physiologists know' (BGE 231). Nietzsche compares the quest for knowledge to the quest for nutrition and explains that human learning is a transformative process that relates back to the physiology of vegetative life. Confronted with the 'basic text *homo natura*', Nietzsche asks anew what the human being is and what it means philosophically that the human being finds itself as a living being, an animal, an organism (Riedel 1996: 205). As such, the affirmation of the 'basic text *homo natura*' inevitably raises the question of sexuality: 'the fundamental problem (*Grundproblem*) "man and woman"' (BGE 238). However, before we can turn to this problem, we need to address the question of how nature relates to transformation and whether knowledge and the pursuit of truth foster human self- transformation.

Nietzsche pursues the kind of knowledge that 'transforms us (*verwandelt uns*)'. But he then seems to suggest that there is something 'at the bottom (*im Grunde*) of us really "deep down (*da unten*)"' which is predetermined, unteachable, and unchangeable, something which is settled and fixed: a granite of spiritual fatum that is inaccessible to and removed from the process of self-transformation (BGE 231). Curiously, Nietzsche pairs the terms that describe the inaccessibility of human nature – 'predetermined (*vorherbestimmt*)', 'unteachable (*unbelehrbar*)', 'unchangeable (*unwandelbar*)' and 'fixed (*fest*)' – with terms that suggest the opposite, namely, the fluidity and mutability of human nature. He speaks of 'decision and answer', 'selected questions', 'solutions to problems', 'steps to self-knowledge' and 'signposts of the problem we are'. All of these terms suggest that the philosophical life is a life of becoming and self-overcoming, of open enquiry and quest for knowledge, a journey of continuous self-discovery where 'the question of "Who we are?" is perpetually answered and yet remains perpetually open' (Owen 1998: 320).

The predetermined, unteachable, unchangeable and fixed in Nietzsche's description of individual nature do not point towards the essence of human nature. Rather, the discovery of *homo natura* comes hand in hand with the affirmation of the limits of knowledge. The problem of nature is that although nature belongs to us and defines us inherently, it is something that we can never fully capture, understand and make our own: '[w]e remain strange to ourselves out of necessity, we do not understand ourselves, we must confusedly mistake who we are, the motto "everyone is furthest from himself" applies to us forever, – we are not "knowers" when it comes to ourselves . . .' (GM 1). This is why in the quest for self-knowledge, we learn by way of error, with provisional solutions and answers – 'convictions' – pointing us towards who we are not. For, strictly speaking, there is nothing that we can learn about who we are. Here, as Nietzsche claims, the thinker can only 'finish learning (*auslernen*)', literally exit learning, and bring their striving for knowledge to a halt (*zu Ende entdecken*) (BGE 231). Here, the learning process hits stone, hence perhaps the reference to granite. The will to truth and its quest for knowledge only get us to a certain point in the pursuit of (self-)transformation and cultural renewal. Ultimately, transformation (*umlernen*) requires unlearning (*auslernen*): reason needs to come to a standstill and acknowledge that in the end, as Nietzsche points out, all cultural achievements are the achievements of nature (HC). They are not the work of reason but the work of nature:

> in the last analysis all thought depends on something unteachable 'deep down', on a fundamental stupidity; the nature of the individual, the individual nature, not evident and universally valid insights, it seems, is the ground of all worthwhile understanding and knowledge. (Strauss 1983: 190)

The limits of reason and the acknowledgement of the cultural force of nature recall Nietzsche's distinction between the Romans and the Greeks and his claim that he learned strictly nothing from the Greeks: they are 'too fluid', 'too inaccessible' (TI 'Ancients'). Perhaps what Nietzsche learned from the Greeks is that, before the overfullness and wealth of nature, we need to '*auslernen* (exit learning)'. Genuine transformation requires not a movement back to nature but a movement up to nature, to a newly discovered naturalness. It means, as Annemarie Pieper has put it, that one understands 'the whole of nature not from the perspective of human self-understanding, but the other way around, human nature from the perspective of the wealth of non-human nature' (Pieper 2012: 60). When Nietzsche places the phrases 'woman as such' and 'deep down' in quotation marks, this functions neither as a reference to the fundamental sexual difference between male and female nor to the 'basic text of species inheritance', as Lampert argues (Lampert 2001: 233). Rather, Nietzsche speaks from the perspective of a will to truth that has thrown off the shackles of morality and reason: 'about man and woman, for example, a thinker cannot relearn (*umlernen*) but only finish learning (*auslernen*) – only discover ultimately how this is "settled in him (*feststeht*)"' (BGE 231). Nietzsche acknowledges his own stupidity, the point where he can only exit learning, not only as a limit of reason and morality but also as an opening towards nature's imaginary which allows the individual to continuously imagine and reimagine, create and recreate its own individual nature, including its sexuality.

'Woman as such', Probity and the Critique of Enlightenment

If the discovery of *homo natura* marks the end of philosophy as the pursuit of absolute truth, then, as Karl Löwith points out, this discovery also forms a new beginning, namely, the emergence of truth as probity. In contrast to readings of *Beyond Good and Evil* that treat Nietzsche's thinking about probity as separate from his conception of sexuality (van Tongeren 2014) or that understand Nietzsche's thinking about 'woman as such' and the 'basic problem of "man and woman"' as an illustration of probity (Clarke 1998; Acampora and Ansell-Pearson 2011), I argue that the emergence of truth as probity comes through the affirmation of the human being as a sexual being. This is true in two distinct senses: from Foucault's perspective, the history of the 'will to truth' has been marked by its descent from pastoral practices of self-examination and confession that he has illustrated in the volumes of the *History of Sexuality*. But these pastoral practices were based on a belief in the radical separateness of the human being from its animal and plant nature, and from a linked construction of sexuality as the object of a government of souls, a disciplinary and biopolitical regimentation of the drives. For Nietzsche, truth as probity attempts to undo this Christian provenance. The project of probity requires an entirely different approach to sexuality and its function in the constitution of human nature. In other words, sexuality provides the key to Nietzsche's understanding of probity.

Just as the discovery of the 'basic text *homo natura*' does not lead Nietzsche to postulate an anthropology, a series of universal validity claims about human nature, nor does it lead him to a scientific or biological reconstruction of human species life, so too his thinking about sexuality is determined by the discovery that 'about man and woman, for example, a thinker cannot relearn (*umlernen*) but only finish learning (*auslernen*) – only discover ultimately how this is "settled in him (*feststeht*)"' (BGE 231). In Nietzsche, the 'truth' that emerges from the problem field of sexual difference (referred to by the ironical expression 'woman as such') is, therefore, not an abstract or anonymous truth, but reflects the thinking of each individual, which is why Nietzsche speaks of '*my* truths' (BGE 231).

According to Derrida, the reference to '*my* truths' indicates that:

> they are not *truth* since they are multiple, multicolored, contradictory. There is therefore no one truth in itself but additionally, even for me, of me, truth is plural. [. . .] There is therefore no truth in itself of sexual difference in itself, of woman or of man [. . .]. (Derrida 1998: 64)

But what is responsible for the fact that there are no absolute and universal truths in the singular, but always only personalised truth ('my') in the plural?[19] Derrida offers as explanation that:

> all the Nietzschean analyses on sexual difference [. . .] all have as vector what could be called the trial or propriation (appropriation, expropriation, hold, possessive hold, gift and exchange, mastery, servitude, etc.) [. . .]. It appeared, according to an already formalized rule, that woman is woman as much in giving, yielding, *in yielding herself*, while man holds and takes, possesses, takes possession, but on the contrary in giving herself woman *yields-as* [gives-herself-for] to dissimulate and assure herself of possessive mastery [. . .] Man and woman trade places, exchange their masks to infinity. (Ibid.: 65)[20]

In other words, Derrida sees in Nietzsche's discussion of 'woman as such' and sexual difference the uncovering of the 'sexual operation' of 'propriation', of turning anything into 'itself', what he would later call 'ipseity', and the ruin of any such ipseity by its constitutive *différance* or inappropiable alterity. But, on this reading, '*my* truths' cannot be what they say they are, 'mine', proper to me as opposed to others. Nietzsche's '*my* truths' about 'woman as such' betray a relation to the improper 'nature' that is common to all human beings.

Because the interpretations of these passages in the Nietzsche scholarship, for the most part, do not heed Derrida's suggestions, they subjectivise the question of woman. Thus, Sommer suggests that Nietzsche's 'preamble of subjectivity', his declared personalisation of his truths at the beginning of the section (BGE 231), reflect Nietzsche's own opinions about the topic of women. Sommer notes that Nietzsche's views on women are inseparable from his 'self-expression (*Selbstdarstellung*)', which is poetic in kind (Sommer 2016: 653). I would add that there is also a performative dimension in Nietzsche's 'truths' about women that is political in kind and astute to the power relations reflected in the play of masks, of different personas and gender roles.[21] Nietzsche's reference to 'woman as such' needs to be read as a polemical reference to Immanuel Kant's *Ding an sich* (ibid.: 652). In contrast to Kant's critical philosophy, Nietzsche's critical endeavours are referenced in quotes: they are decidedly subjective and perspectival, reflecting Nietzsche's human, all too human truths on women. Paul van Tongeren adds that this polemic against Kant also extends to Nietzsche's view on virtue. Virtue in Nietzsche is always individual virtue and not a duty that can be universalised as in Kant.

While I agree with Sommer and van Tongeren on Nietzsche's disagreements with Kant, Nietzsche's ironical employment of the '*an sich*' in relation to the question of woman may have also been directed against Kant's thinking about sexuality in his *Anthropology*. There, Kant subsumes the 'characterization of this sex' to 'nature's end in establishing womankind' (Kant 2006: 207), which is a twofold aim. First, through a gendering of sexual difference such that women are by nature weaker in order that 'this sex rightfully demands male protection for itself', nature pursues its end of the preservation of the species. Second, nature's aim is also the 'cultivation of society and its refinement by womankind'. To attain this aim, nature makes 'this sex man's ruler through her modesty and eloquence in speech and expression' such that her claim to 'gentle and courteous treatment by the male' leads him 'if not to morality itself, to that which is its cloak, moral decency' (ibid.). Nietzsche's bringing together an anti-moral probity with regard to the real purpose of moral values, together with a discussion of the 'spurring operation' (Derrida 1979) that Nietzsche sets at work through the question of 'woman as such', tears through this 'cloak' of moral decency. Whereas Kant naturalises sexual difference for the sake of the pragmatic education of humanity, Nietzsche sexualises the nature of humankind in order to spur it beyond itself. Whereas Kant's references to the sexuality of the human being are embedded within the broader project of his anthropology, in Nietzsche, sexuality decentres anthropological constructions of human nature. This is the reason, in my view, why the pluralisation of singular truths in Nietzsche is inseparable from the renaturalisation of philosophy as the becoming of probity. The discovery of *homo natura* and the affirmation of the human being as a sexual being have therefore serious implications for our understanding of philosophy and the will to truth.

In my view, the pluralisation of singular truths thematised by Derrida's reading is a direct result of Nietzsche's naturalisation of philosophy and his affirmation of sexuality. This may explain why in *Beyond Good and Evil* 231, Nietzsche locates the singularity or spiritual *fatum* of the individual in the body as opposed to in the mind. More specifically, the 'granite of spiritual *fatum*' is located 'deep down (*da unten*)' in vegetative life, that is, that aspect of life that is known for its capacity for metamorphosis, reproduction and growth as discussed in Chapter 3. The thinker committed to probity acknowledges that transformation and future generation are contingent on finding the right nourishment and the right type of knowledge, and of choosing the right growing ground and climate (BGE 231, SE 1, also EH).

According to Löwith, the pursuit of truth as probity is reflected in the way in which the philosopher engages with their life and thought, experiencing and experimenting with their life as a continuous commitment to the pursuit of greater (self-)knowledge and self-transformation. As such, truth as probity is historically situated and leads to an inevitable confrontation of the philosopher with their time. Nietzsche's critique of Enlightenment and the gender politics of his time in *Beyond Good and Evil* 231–9 needs to be understood within his more general disagreement with the Christian worldview and its conception of human nature.

Aphorisms 231–9 reflect Nietzsche's standpoint on sexuality and gender in opposition to Christian morality and its denial of sexuality. From the perspective of Nietzsche's critique, the Enlightenment stands under the rule of morality over the will to truth and as such comes with the denial of life and sexuality – in particular, the sexuality of women. Nietzsche sees in the Enlightenment ideal of the emancipated woman, in 'attempts of women at scientific self-exposure (*weibliche Wissenschaftlichkeit*)' (BGE 232), 'feminine vainglory (*weibliche Selbstherrlichkeit*)', a symptom of 'corruption of the instincts' (BGE 233).

The instincts at issue are figured by Nietzsche in terms of 'biological metaphors – womb of being, mother eternally pregnant, procreative life' (Oliver 1998: 76). These metaphors, more than symptoms of Nietzsche's view that 'woman is permanently sexually motivated, but always with the end in view of pregnancy' (Diethe 1996: 60), rather indicate that what is at stake in Nietzsche's critique of women's emancipation along the lines of equal rights, is his opposition to the Enlightenment's naturalisation of sexual difference through the sexualisation of nature. Building on Derrida's distinction between the castrated, castrating and affirming women, Kelly Oliver offers an interpretation of what Nietzsche may intend with his discourse on the corruption (in her language 'castration') of instincts. On her reading, the

> castrated woman is the feminist who uses the will to truth either to enhance survival or dominate life. The castrating woman is the artist who uses the will to illusion either to playfully affirm the multiplicity of life or cunningly deceive us in order to gain advantage. The affirming woman is the will to power which either creates or destroys life. (Oliver 1998: 68)

Oliver argues that the castrated woman is the most tyrannical because she denies women and affirms herself as man. The castrating woman is the actor who runs the risk of believing in her own illusion. By contrast, the affirming woman has no need for truth: she affirms herself without man and logocentrism (ibid.: 76). The 'Dionysian woman affirms herself outside of the metaphysic of truth. She is will to power, the original mother, eternally pregnant' (ibid.: 78).

I return below to this figure of the Dionysian mother. For the moment, my concern is with Nietzsche's opposition between, on the one hand, the affirmation of women's creative and procreative instincts, women as a cultural force of transformation and future generation, and, on the other hand, the emancipated women who compromise their claims to develop a singular nature and instead adopt the values of the Enlightenment. Nietzsche observes that 'Woman (*Weib*) wants to become self-reliant (*selbst-ständig*): and for that reason, she is beginning to enlighten men about "woman as such"' and sees this as 'one of the worst developments (*schlimmsten Fortschritten*) of the general *uglification* of Europe' (BGE 232). Enlightenment leads to the 'odd symptom (*merkwürdigen Symptom*) of the increasing weakening and dulling (*Abstumpfung*) of the most feminine (*allerweiblichsten*) instincts' (BGE 239).

Nietzsche deploys multiple meanings of the term 'stupidity (*Dummheit*)' to illustrate the shortcomings of the false Enlightenment ideal of emancipation. In contrast, in aphorism 231, Nietzsche affirms his own stupidity as a source of truth and cultural productivity, a stupidity which, I add, may qualify as animal and feminine. By contrast, in aphorism 239 stupidity takes on the opposite meaning, namely as a reference to a lack of creativity in the relation to one's own nature that is distinctly masculine and inherent to the Enlightenment movement: 'There is *stupidity* in this movement, an almost masculine stupidity of which a woman who has turned out well (*wohlgerathenes Weib*) – and such women are always prudent (*kluges*) – would have to be thoroughly (*von Grund aus*) ashamed' (BGE 239). Nietzsche calls out for women not to copy the stupidity of those men who adhere to the Enlightenment ideal according to which greater knowledge also means greater freedom: 'to imitate all the stupidities with which "men" in Europe, European "manliness" in Europa, is sick' (BGE 239).

When Nietzsche claims that women should be ashamed of imitating the stupidity of men, he is not adopting a Christian conception of shame. The latter is part of those discourses that make women sick: 'almost everywhere one ruins her nerves with the most pathological and dangerous music [. . .] and makes her more hysterical by the day and more incapable of her first and last profession – to give birth to strong children' (BGE 239).[22] Nietzsche is all too aware of the fact that instilling shame is a means of domination. By contrast, Nietzsche refers to the Greek idea of shame as an antidote against the drive to knowledge. The Greeks knew how to ignore, to be stupid, to stop at the surface, admiring the beauty of nature rather than penetrating and destroying it: 'One should have more respect (*in Ehren halten*) for the bashfulness (*Scham*) with which nature has hidden behind riddles and iridescent (*bunte*) uncertainties' (GS Preface 4).

This moment of Nietzsche's argument, so dependent on the Greek idea of shame as the veiling of 'the raw force of the womb of life' (Oliver 1998: 79), has been linked by feminist interpreters to the mythical figure of Baubô. Sarah Kofman argues that Nietzsche seeks to reintroduce an ancient Greek conception of women exemplified by the figure of Baubô in the myth of Demeter, who makes the goddess of fertility laugh again after the loss of her daughter Persephone, and rejoice again in her femininity (Kofman 1998). Nietzsche revives an ancient idea of nature associated with mother earth and the suffering and sacrifice involved in creative processes. Commenting on one version of the story of Baubô, according to which Demeter only starts to laugh when Baubô 'lifts her skirt and shows her genitals with the laughing baby Iakchos (another name for Dionysus) who has his hand under her breast', Sigridur Thorgeirsdottir has argued that

[I]t is possible that there is something transgender about Baubô [. . .] she may have displayed body parts that are not womanly, i.e. male-like genitalia. So in light of all this Baubô and Dionysus are both Dionysian in the sense of being deities that refer to the earth, and life as giving and taking, birth and death. Yet they also represent a form of sexual difference as Baubô is a woman and Dionysus is a man, despite their transgender features. In that sense, sexual difference is not something static, endowing the sexes with innate differences, but rather something that is becoming and changing. (Thorgeirsdottir 2012: 70)[23]

Nietzsche invites women to celebrate their sexuality – in particular, their capacity to ensure the future of generations – instead of imitating the stupidity of men. In this view, women are both the subjects and objects of a dialectic of Enlightenment where a desire for greater freedom and independence ends up producing greater forms of domination. Nietzsche's critique of modernity and his aspiration for cultural renewal seeks to reverse these modern developments. Nietzsche may be 'the real friend of women (*rechter Weiberfreund*)', counselling them not to compromise themselves through the Enlightenment (BGE 232). This is why Pieper reads Nietzsche's views on women as an encouragement for women to embrace their sexuality, empowering them to take a position against male domination. She argues that Nietzsche invites each and every individual to decide:

> where each and every one draws for themselves the line between sex and gender and to think about meaningful ways in which we can support our natural inclinations and change social conceptions of sexuality, instead of engaging in an unfruitful fight against the 'granite' of our first nature. (Pieper 2012: 63)

Pieper's reading posits a standpoint from which the Dionysian sexualisation of nature makes it thinkable to transform not only gender but also the materiality of sexuality and sexual difference. However, this standpoint still identifies sexual difference as a fatality of 'first nature' that may be compensated by 'second nature' (that is, culture and society) but is not yet seen as the source of all cultural and social creativity.

When Nietzsche situates sexual difference beyond the reach of knowledge, this is not an aspect of his so-called essentialism about sexual difference. Instead, it reflects his belief that singular nature lies beyond the reach of civilisation and the processes of education:

> They would like to reduce (*herunterbringen*) women to the level of 'general education' [. . .] Altogether one wants to make her more 'cultivated' and, as is said, make the weaker sex strong through culture: as if history did not teach us as impressively as possible that making the human being more 'cultivated' and making them weak – weakening, splintering and sickling of the force of the will, have always kept pace, and that the most powerful and influential women of the world (most recently Napoleon's mother) owed their power and ascendency (*Übergewicht*) over men to the force of their will – not to the schoolmasters! (BGE 239)

The idea that singularity is situated beyond the reach of civilisation can already be found in *Schopenhauer as Educator*, where Nietzsche speaks of the individual as singular and without comparison (SE 1). In this early work, Nietzsche argues, very much in line with Emerson, that if we desire to become who we are, we need to remind ourselves of our irreducible singularity or higher nature as a force that allows us to resist the conformism of our time. The irreducible singularity of each and every individual, however, is not the mark of some sort of essentialism about human nature. Rather, our singular nature reflects a cultural force (here the youth of a generation) that allows us to overcome the errors of civilisation and reimagine a 'more natural' culture (SE 1).

Nietzsche advocates for education as a liberating and truly transformative experience where the individual embraces singularity as a destiny that obliges the individual to take position and responsibility for the becoming of who they are (SE 1). Nietzsche's conception of singularity as destiny is therefore not ontological or biological but cultural and political. In the case of the philosopher committed to probity as Nietzsche envisages her, her singular nature and destiny obliges her to take position publicly on the question of human nature. After all, this is what probity alludes to: the courage to speak the truth publicly and before others. Probity is in this respect a philosophical–political virtue that Nietzsche situates 'beyond good and evil' and beyond the political ideologies of his time.

The Enlightenment promises a false liberation for women; it abuses the idea of respect for women: 'this respect is immediately abused' (BGE 239).[24] As a consequence, '*woman is retrogressing (das Weib geht zurück)*' (BGE 239). By contrast, what inspires respect of women, and often enough even fear, is her *nature*, which is more 'natural (*natürlicher*)' than man's:

> the genuine cunning suppleness of a beast of prey (*echte, raubthierhafte listige Geschmeidigkeit*), the tiger's claw under the glove, the naïveté of her egoism, her uneducatability (*Unerziehbarkeit*) and inner wildness, the incomprehensibility, scope and movement of her desires (*Begierden*) and virtues . . . (BGE 239)

In contrast to the Enlightenment's emancipatory ideal of the human being as something distinct and 'higher' than nature, Nietzsche seeks to re-establish the otherness of nature, here the 'more "natural"' naturalness of women, as worthy of respect, and as a source of cultural renewal.

At this point, Nietzsche's sexualisation of nature flows back into a discussion of women as nature, based on the analogy between women and animals. Interestingly, this analogy is supported by the strange coincidence of opposites: wildness and tameness, freedom and restriction. Thus, women are understood to be 'more refined, vulnerable, wilder, stranger, sweeter, and more soulful' animals than men, and therefore 'as something one has to lock up lest it fly away' (BGE 237). The image of women as fearsome animals that have been caught in the social trappings of a male-centred, patriarchal form of civilisation elicits Nietzsche's pity:

> What, in spite of all fear, elicits pity for this dangerous and beautiful cat 'woman'[25] is that she appears to suffer more, to be more vulnerable, more in need of love, and more condemned to disappointment than any other animal. Fear and pity: with these feelings man has so far confronted woman, always with one foot in tragedy which tears to pieces as it enchants. What? And this should be the end? And the breaking of women's magic spell (*Entzauberung des Weibes ist im Werke*)? The borification of women is slowly dawning? (BGE 239)

It is important to note that the idea of woman as nature or naturalness threatened by male civilisation and patriarchal society is a concept that can already be found in Schiller and his sentimental conception of nature. However, whereas in Schiller nature is ethical and makes us more ethical (Riedel 1996: 180–1), in Nietzsche nature becomes distinctly anti-moral. Hence, when Nietzsche writes about the 'Eternal-Feminine' in reference to Goethe (BGE 237),[26] commentators have pointed out that he surely knows this to be a mystification (van Tongeren 2014). Van Tongeren considers Nietzsche's thinking about women to be extra-moral and, as such, neither boring, that is, moralising, nor demystifying, that is, rationalising. According to van Tongeren, Nietzsche seeks to counteract boredom as an integral feature of moral philosophy: 'may I be forgiven the discovery that all moral philosophy so far has been boring' (BGE 227). Likewise, the cultural renewal of Europe is to counteract the Enlightenment movement and the subjection of women to the danger of borification and demystification (BGE 239). For van Tongeren, Nietzsche's use of mockery and parody, such as in aphorism 236 and in the 'Seven Epigrams on Women' (BGE 237), are strategies against the demystification and borification of women as well as against attempts to paint moral virtues over their naturalness. The question is whether Nietzsche's style, his mockery and parody in regards to human sexuality, may not qualify as distinctly Cynic.

Sexuality, Biopolitics and Social Transformation

Aphorism *Beyond Good and Evil* 238 explains that Nietzsche's attack on the modern Enlightenment's presumption in favour of equality, including equality between sexes (Acampora and Ansell-Pearson 2011: 165), is due to his belief that the drive to equality undermines 'the basic problem "man and woman"' by denying the 'most abysmal antagonism' between the sexes, 'the necessity of an eternally hostile tension' (BGE 238):

> [. . .] to dream perhaps of equal rights, equal education, equal claims and obligations: that is a *typical* sign of shallowness, and a thinker who has proved shallow in this dangerous place – shallow in his instincts! [. . .] probably he will be too 'short' for all fundamental problems (*Grundfragen*) of life, of the life yet to come, too, and incapable of attaining *any* depth. (BGE 238)

The 'basic problem "man and woman"' is the last in a series of basic problems that Nietzsche discusses in 'Our Virtues', Chapter 7 of *Beyond Good and Evil*. It concludes Nietzsche's discussion of human nature by introducing a third, explicitly political element, in the relationship between the human being and nature. It raises the question of what does the 'basic problem "man and woman"' mean for each and every individual, for our cultural self-understanding and the ways in which we relate to others and organise ourselves politically?

If the 'shallow' approach to the social organisation of sexual difference takes as its fundamental principle the idea of equality between the sexes, Nietzsche claims that:

> A man who has depth, in his mind as well as in his desires [. . .] must always think about woman as *Orientals* do. He must conceive of woman as a possession, as property that can be locked, as something predestined for service and achieving her perfection in that. Here, he must base himself on the tremendous reason of Asia, on Asia's superiority in the instincts, as the Greeks did formerly, who were Asia's best heirs and students: as is well known, from Homer's time to the age of Pericles, as their culture *increased* along with the range of their powers, they also gradually became more *severe*, in brief more oriental, against woman. How necessary, how logical, how humanely desirable even, this was – is worth pondering on! (BGE 238)

Diethe places this late passage in connection with Nietzsche's earlier essay from 1871, *The Greek Woman*, where he states that 'the Hellenic woman as *mother* had to live in obscurity, because the political instinct together with its highest aim demanded it. She *had* to vegetate like a plant, in the narrow circle, as a symbol of the Epicurean wisdom' (as cited by Diethe 1996: p. 41). For Diethe, this means that Nietzsche advocated that 'women should be closeted away' and relegated to a 'domestic role' (Diethe 1996: 42–3).

In this context, it seems important to take a view of these passages that bring them in conversation with Rubin's text on the 'political economy of "sex"' (Rubin 1975) as much as with Hannah Arendt's reflections on why sex and sexuality was kept in the relative 'darkness' of the *oikos* (Arendt 1958). Nietzsche's passage, with its reference to women being a 'possession', 'locked' in the household and 'predestined for service', not only seems to refer to the situation in Greece when the patriarchal hold on power was strongest and also coincided with the most radical separation of the dimensions of the *polis* and those of the *oikos*, but also contradicts the main social transformation in his own society which saw masses of women leave the house to join the workforce. And yet, precisely the reference to Asia, and the reference to Greece as 'Asia's best heirs and students', leaves open the possibility of a more complicated reading of this passage. The reason is that the cult of Dionysus – a divinity associated with women and servants/slaves, that is, a divinity of the members of the household, who is worshipped, however, outside of the *oikos*, in the forests, together with wild animals – was adopted by the Greeks from the 'Orient'. Given Nietzsche's later elaborations on Dionysus and Ariadne as symbolic for his understanding of 'the basic problem of "man" and "woman"', it is possible that in this passage Nietzsche may be drawing the bow, Apollo's instrument, in an Apollonian direction only to let his arrow fly in the opposite direction.

Sommer argues that in this passage Nietzsche reflects on how men have treated women in the past and poses the question of how men will treat women in the future (Sommer 2016: 666). Will men continue to oppress women, as suggested by

Nietzsche's description of the past treatment of women as birds that are kept in cages? Or will men treat women as their equal, as Nietzsche's description of the democratisation of European culture seems to suggest? Whereas Sommer asks the question of how Nietzsche envisages the future renewal of European culture and society from the perspective of men – the *Andros*, that is, 'will men treat . . .', as if women were objects that men relate to at will – I propose posing this question from the perspective of a newly discovered naturalness. From this perspective, the question is whether social life can become again an expression of the creativity of natural life, or, to the contrary, whether social life will continue to institute barriers between the human being (*homo*) and nature (*natura*). I therefore suggest bringing to bear a biopolitical perspective on this passage, so that the question is whether society is a barrier against natural life, or, instead, whether it becomes a facilitator of the cultural productivity of nature.

As Esposito has lately argued, following the indications of Foucault's analytic of biopower, Nietzsche's critique of Enlightenment suggests that modern society has erected a barrier between the human being and nature by protecting and immunising the human being against it (Esposito 2011). Nietzsche's discussion of equal rights suggests that, in his view, the separation of the human being (women) from nature, by bringing women out of the household and into the public sphere, may have worsened the situation of women in society: '[s]ince the French Revolution, woman's influence in Europe has decreased proportionately as her rights and claims have increased' (BGE 239). Instead of increasing women's standing in society, liberal equal rights have disempowered women by decreasing their influence. The so-called 'progress (*Fortschritt*)' of the modern age has had the opposite consequence for women. The logic here is similar to that found in Alexis de Tocqueville or Søren Kierkegaard. Tocqueville (2003) argues that it is precisely by withdrawing from the democratic political process that religion retains its greatest authority and power, something that it loses as soon as it intervenes into the public sphere directly. Analogously, Kierkegaard (1962) argues that the modern, democratic sphere is necessarily levelling and generative of resentment towards anything high or great. As a consequence, anyone who wishes to pursue something of high value must do so in secret or anonymously, and in any case far from the glare of the public sphere. It is possible that one element in Nietzsche's apparently 'conservative' recommendation for women to 'remain at home' may be rather to shield them from such a levelling effect that would disempower them from effecting the needed cultural transformation, which is that of bringing down the barriers between society and nature more than those between private and public spheres.

For Nietzsche, and despite Sommer's suggestion, the question is therefore not one of choosing between two forms of domination – woman as possessions (ancient) or woman as equals (modern).[27] Rather, Nietzsche conceives of social relations, in particular the relation between men and women in the sphere of social reproduction, as the true place of human creativity. That is, Nietzsche calls for the application of creativity to the recreation of sexualised and gendered social roles, something that would occur at the personal–political level of sexual and affective relations, as the main way to explode normative heterosexuality from the inside, as it were. Under the name of Dionysus, Nietzsche advances a vision of social relations that are free and creative based on an affirmation of sexuality as a cultural force of transformation and future generation. In my view, the discovery of *homo natura* leads Nietzsche to postulate social relationships as inherently creative and transformative.

In Nietzsche's views on sexuality, one can therefore distinguish a biopolitics of domination, where sexuality functions as a dispositive of domination, and an affirmative biopolitics where sexuality is no longer bound up with preconceived ideas of gender and sex, but instead opens the horizons of social imaginaries of liberation and creative transformation. To capture the elements of Nietzsche's affirmative biopolitics, and the reason why his placement of women in the household, far from depoliticising the role of women, to the contrary, situates them at the very heart of modern biopower, it is helpful to review the context of the nineteenth-century discourses on the sexualisation of nature and the socialisation of sexuality. Nietzsche's discussion of the 'basic problem "man and woman"' best illustrates this new development in literary and philosophical anthropology in the nineteenth century, namely, that since 1900 literary anthropology conceives human nature through a new discourse on animality, drives and passions. At the centre of this new understanding of human nature stands the human body and sexuality: 'Literary modernism negotiates the nature of the human being through the body' (Riedel 1996: 154).[28] The paradigm shift towards the body and its sexuality in the understanding of the nature of the human being reflects the entry of biological science as the new episteme of the nineteenth century: 'In view of gaining a better understanding of what life is, the new biological sciences increasingly centre their anthropology on an investigation of the body and its sexuality' (ibid.: 165). What marks this paradigm shift in biology is the discovery of reproduction and sexuality – in particular, in the metamorphosis of the plant – that leads to a new understanding of nature as living nature and hence of the human being as a living being with reproduction as the key feature of life (ibid.: 159–60). Nature is living nature to the extent that it grows and reproduces itself out of itself: 'As soon as the new life sciences approach the phenomenon of life as a system of self-production, their central focus is on bisexual reproduction, on Sexuality' (ibid.: 160). In this paradigm, plants, animals and humans share the same mechanism of reproduction (sexuality) that can be traced all the way to the life of individual cells. For Riedel, the life sciences of Nietzsche's time confirm that nature is in becoming, the continuous flow and exchange of cells, and that self-production is nothing but a continuous death where death becomes an instance of life and vice versa. Life is both creation and destruction, sensuality and cruelty, Eros and Thanatos (ibid.: 206). What stands in the foreground is no longer simply the life of the individual and its striving for self-preservation. Rather, the latter needs to be understood as an instance of the life of the species and its drive for preservation.

According to Riedel, this new anthropology finds one of its first iterations in Schopenhauer's philosophy of the will and the view that '[. . .] the human being is [like every plant and every animal] concretely sex drive (*Geschlechtstrieb*). [. . .] the sex drive is the fullest expression of the will to life' (as cited by Riedel 1996: 172). For Schopenhauer, growth, reproduction and metamorphoses are vital and vegetative processes that pertain to plant, animal and human life and that are entirely unrelated to '*Erkenntnis* (knowledge)', an idea which resonates with Nietzsche's discussion of 'the granite of spiritual *fatum*' and the idea that nature is inaccessible and unknowable, presented earlier. The vegetative process of life exemplifies nature as 'teleology *without* consciousness, regularity (*Zweckmäßigkeit*) without knowledge, "order ('completeness') without spirit" – herein lies for Schopenhauer the *mysterium tremendum* of "nature as life", that he tries to capture through the concept of "world as will" (*Welt als Wille*) (*sive sexus*)' (Riedel 1996: 176). In the notion of the will, Schopenhauer attempts to grasp the strangeness and otherness of nature within the human intellect, and as something that is active and creative in all organic processes. Again, this idea is also reflected in the naturalisation of philosophy and the attempt to understand human nature from the perspective of the otherness of nature in Nietzsche.

The affinities between Schopenhauer's philosophy of the will and Nietzsche's philosophy of life have been the subject of many discussions: both provide examples of what I have been referring to as the sexualisation of nature in the nineteenth century.[29] However, what is new with Nietzsche, and what distinguishes his treatment of sexuality from that of Schopenhauer, is the way in which he takes up the socialisation of sexuality in the nineteenth century in his thinking about 'the basic problem "man and woman"'. Sommer observes that Nietzsche's thinking about the role of women in society may have been influenced by August Bebel's *Die Frau in der Vergangenheit, Gegenwart und Zukunft* (1883). Bebel argues that the quintessence of the role of women in society is reflected in their economic dependence, their slavish subjection to men. Sommer claims that this idea of economic dependence is visible in Nietzsche's conception of women as a property that can be used and subsequently traded, best exemplified by the status of women in antiquity (Sommer 2016: 667). Contrary to Nietzsche, Bebel argues for the liberation of women by means of economic independence and access to education (ibid.: 670). Nietzsche, in contrast, appeals to 'fear and pity' as the key forces that bind women and men to each other. Like van Tongeren, Sommer also notes that these are the emotions that tragedy triggers in the spectator, according to Aristotle's theory. He concludes that Nietzsche conceives of the relationship among men and women as tragic, an idea found in some of Nietzsche's later texts, where he speaks of the presentation of the relationship among sexes and of love in Georges Bizet's *Carmen* as exemplarily tragic (ibid.: 671).

Sommer's interpretation seems to mix up ancient and modern conceptions of possession and associated conceptions of male–female relationships. In my view, Nietzsche's critique of the modern idea of marriage is not unlike that of Karl Marx: both suspect beneath the marriage contract a form of domination that gives men power over women, that is, makes women their possession.[30] The contract of marriage supposedly establishes man and woman as equals and as such undermines the 'most abysmal antagonism' between the sexes, 'the necessity of an eternally hostile tension' (BGE 238). This hostility between men and women, and nothing else, is in reality the *Ur-text* to which Nietzsche refers as the 'tragic' form of the 'basic problem of "man and woman"', as any perusal of Greek tragedies confirms.

Nietzsche upholds the antagonism and tension between man and woman, but this does not mean that he is an advocate of sexual dualism. Rather, Nietzsche's conception of the war between the sexes needs to be read against the background of ancient and archaic conceptions of nature. Pieper convincingly argues that nature in Nietzsche has a strong affinity with Heraclitus's understanding of nature as that which grows, accomplishes itself and decays without any contribution of the human being. Nature is uninterrupted becoming, something that gives rise to itself out of itself. The underlying force of nature's eternal cycle of life is the contest or war between opposites, as in the war between the sexes. These opposites, however, are not conceived as absolutes but as shifting and open-ended. It is a transformative relationship rather than a fixed dualism between opposing poles. Hence, oppositions are never strict or absolute but rather transitory and themselves in movement. Against the background of the Heraclitean conception of nature, Pieper argues that the 'basic problem "man and woman"' does not point to an absolute difference between sexes but rather to differences in degrees (Pieper 2012: 61). For me the key is that sexual difference arises out of a relationship, a productive tension or *agon* between 'man and woman', and as such undermines any attempt to conceive their relationship as one between opposite binary poles. Nietzsche is thus concerned with the plurality of differences and not 'this' difference between man and woman.

Riedel also finds in Nietzsche's reflections on sexuality the effects of an ancient conception of nature. At first sight this may seem counterintuitive, given the influence of modern biology on his thinking about human nature. However, Riedel argues as part of his broader analysis of literary and philosophical anthropology in the nineteenth century that the new discourse on human nature does not reflect a new alliance between literature and science; on the contrary, the reception of biology in literature and philosophy leads to a new alliance between them that preserves a non-scientistic conception of nature in modernity (Riedel 1996: xiv). Riedel finds the latter exemplified in both Nietzsche's and Bachofen's theories of the socialisation of sexuality. Riedel compares Nietzsche's understanding of male–female relationships with Bachofen's conception of matriarchy:

> Nietzsche's enthusiastic depiction of 'intoxication (*Rausch*)' and 'Spring', in other words, the fertility and vegetation cults of the early Greeks, which here represent 'archaic human beings and people' (and who are thus described as 'natural human beings (*Naturmenschen*)' in 'the Dionysian worldview'), may have a much stronger affinity with Bachofen's image of antiquity than what one may have expected given the systematic blurring of tracks and denial of sources during the lifetime of Nietzsche's published works. (Ibid.: 186)[31]

Riedel argues that with Bachofen, the sentimental and moral depiction of women as 'more natural' that was found in Schiller becomes more sexual in the form of his recovery of the organisation of matriarchy as the golden age of humanity: 'The paradisiac of the Saturnine world peace results from motherhood, by contrast chaos is the result of female *eros* and unbound sexuality' (ibid.: 183). With Nietzsche's adoption and adaptation of Bachofen, in particular with the figure of the Satyr as a reflection of human–animal–sexual nature, nature is definitely broken free from its association with humanity and morality, as in Schiller's sentimental and naïve mystification (*Verklärung*) of women as nature (ibid.: 191).

The sexualisation of nature in Nietzsche is reflected in the Dionysian as the symbol for eternal life:

> This is why for the Greeks the sexual symbol was considered to be the most honourable symbol, where ancient piety finds its deepest meaning. All the details of the act of procreation, pregnancy, and birth, stir up the most solemn feelings in the Greek. [. . .] All this is reflected in the word Dionysus: I know

of no higher symbolic than this Greek symbolic [. . .] the deepest instinct for life, for the future of life, for the eternity of life is reflected in this symbolism and is experienced religiously as the pathway to Life, to procreation, as the holy pathway . . . (KSA 13:14[89].266)

Dionysus is Nietzsche's answer to the denial of sexuality in the Christian worldview which, according to Nietzsche, commits a crime against humanity precisely by destroying this religious feeling and appreciation of nature and sexuality as a 'holy pathway' to the future generation of humanity.

The biopolitical dimension of Nietzsche's thinking about sexuality and gender requires bringing together both the sexualisation of nature and the socialisation of nature characteristic of nineteenth-century anthropological discourse. First of all, for Nietzsche, the 'basic problem of "man and woman"' is clearly a political problem, a question of life and death conflict, but one that explodes 'at home' so to speak, hence the irony and appropriateness of the 'old' woman's suggestion to Zarathustra: when thinking about women, do not forget to 'bring the whip'. With Nietzsche, and in contrast to Lampert's suggestion, the relation between male and female can no longer be considered merely a domestic one: it is at once economic (belonging to the *oikos*) and political. According to Lampert, echoing Baeumler, Nietzsche's praise of Greek heroism begins 'at home':

Greek male contest, Nietzsche seems to suggest, began at home with the most domestic, began with a man's estimation of woman and the womanly insofar as they represented the basic will of the mind. For a male given to context, the female was a recreation, an occasion for play, but something both more delicate and more wild, something that had strayed from some height and had to be locked up lest it be lost. (Lampert 2001: 238)

In Lampert, this domestic *agon* culminates in the harmony between the sexes, 'in [the] productive union, as told in poetic tales of the manly and the womanly, of Zarathustra and Life, of Dionysus and Ariadne' (ibid.: 233), where the marriage between Dionysus and Ariadne 'composes the sexual difference into a fecund harmony' (ibid.: 242). In contrast to Lampert's depiction of the relationship between Dionysus and Ariadne as an example of the ideal (bourgeois) marriage, I suggest a closer examination of Bachofen and the idea of possession associated with his conception of matriarchy. For Bachofen, pre-matriarchal times stand under the rule of the primordial horde, where women could be taken by anyone to the extent that women were no one's possession. Here it is also useful to recall that for Derrida the question of 'woman as such' in the end amounts to the problem of 'propriation' and its impossibility, that is, the impossibility of sexual difference to lend itself to the once and for all appropriation of the women by the men. For Bachofen, it is the political and social institution of matriarchy that puts an end to the rule of the primordial horde over women by introducing marriage as an arrangement where women become the possession of the family and are charged with the future generation of human life (Bachofen 1861). This matriarchal meaning of marriage and possession is thus entirely different from the patriarchal sense of 'possession' discussed by Rubin (1975) and Shulamith Firestone (2003), where women become objects that belong to men and can be exchanged among men like gifts or commodities. The key of the matriarchal idea of possession is that it is an expression of the power and freedom of women.

Interestingly, according to the findings of Kyle Harper (2017: 111) and Orlando Patterson, the Greek word for freedom, *eleuthera*, in its most archaic sense refers to 'a free woman', that is, a 'sexually respectable woman' or a woman 'with a claim to sexual honor' (Patterson 2017: 283). Patterson adds that it could also mean 'wife'. These meanings coincide with the ones Bachofen associates with matriarchy, not patriarchy. The basic argument offered by Harper and Patterson is that the possession of socially recognised and publicly protected sexual honour was an essential part of the experience of personal freedom for women in the ancient world (ibid.). Paterson recalls that:

> the civic dimension of *eleuthera* – which Greek men were to construct as democracy –lay dormant in the most primeval meaning of the word, 'because the capacity to reproduce the city was embedded at the heart of what it meant to be a free woman in the ancient Mediterranean'. (Patterson 2017: 283, citing Harper 2017)

By reminding modern women of the Dionysian, 'Asian' link between naturalness, sexuality and political power, Nietzsche may well have sought to give back to women the kind of power and respect they once held in the memory of the ancient world. This power is not just about reproduction but about the combining of control over reproduction (the decision of when and with whom to reproduce) with the political power that characterises matriarchy.

I conclude with a few thoughts on the ancient Cynics and suggest that perhaps Nietzsche's vision of the future philosopher committed to probity finds its precursor in the ancient Cynics' affirmation of sexuality and their respect for women. It is thanks to the late Foucault that we can appreciate the political and philosophical importance of the Cynics' way of life: they were the first who understood truth as lived and embodied truth (Foucault 2011; Goulet-Cazé 2014). They were also among the first who contested the division between public and private, citizens and slaves, man and woman as means of domination and oppression of nature, as barriers set up to protect the human being against nature, including its own nature. To overthrow these barriers, the Cynics enacted a return to nature, an embodiment of nature, where nature is conceived as a creative and artistic force. In my view, the Cynics strove towards an idea of community where social relationships, including that between man and women, were affirmed and lived as artefacts of nature (Lemm 2014a). The Cynics are the antiheros of the history of philosophy who celebrate their 'going under (*Untergang*)' and decline as a 'going over (*Übergang*)' to a new idea of community where man and woman are equals and share everything in common, as illustrated by the marriage between Crates and Hipparchia. Cynic love is a higher form of love. Perhaps this is because in the Cynics, the role of nature and sexuality in a future society is affirmed as creative and artistic, as feminine and 'the Eternal-Feminine' (BGE 236). In this view, the true social function of art is no longer reflected in the hero's life, male, but rather in the downfall of all heroism which corresponds to art as the creation of society, female:

> For what must be clear to us above all, both to our humiliation and our elevation, is that the whole comedy of art is certainly not performed for us, neither for our edification nor our education, just as we are far from truly being the creators of that

world of art; conversely, however, we may very well assume we are already images and artistic projections for the true creator of art, and that our highest dignity lies in our significance as works of art. (BT 5)

Notes

1 'There is no essence to woman because woman separates and separates from and of herself. She submerges, veils through the depths, without end, without ground, all essentiality, all identity, all propriety. Blinded here, philosophical discourse plummets, left to plunge to its ruin. There is no truth to woman but it's because this abyssal separation of truth, this nontruth is the "truth". Woman is the name for this nontruth of truth' (Derrida 1998: 53).

2 Annemarie Pieper correctly notes that for Nietzsche through the sexual organs, 'the human being is indissolubly and eternally chained to the organic world' (Pieper 2012: 61). As Nietzsche puts it: 'The abdomen (*Unterleib*) is the reason why the human being does not easily take itself for a god' (BGE 141).

3 Butler's critique of Rubin's 'revolution in kinship' is based on the claim that Rubin 'maintains that before the transformation of a biological male or female into a gendered man or woman "each child contains all of the sexual possibilities available to human expression"' (Butler 1999: 94). Butler applies Foucault's lesson to point out 'the illusion of a sexuality before the law is itself the creation of that law' (ibid.).

4 Carol Diethe (1996), who argues for Nietzsche's misogyny, nonetheless agrees with Annemarie Pieper that 'the whip referred to could belong to the woman to be visited just as plausibly as to the visiting man. Pieper teases out a further possible meaning by suggesting that the woman might be acting in the role of supervisor to make sure that the man fulfils his destiny of striving to become the *Übermensch*. The whip could then, just possibly, be seen as "a symbol for self-overcoming"' (Diethe 1996: 64, citing Pieper 1990: 312).

5 'The sexual drive exists as an essential condition of life and of the foundation of society. It is the strongest drive in human nature. Whatever becomes extinct, this drive perseveres. Undeveloped, not an object of

thought, but nevertheless the central fire of life, this inescapable drive is the natural protection against every type of destruction' (Bebel 1883: 38, cited in Sommer 2016: 656).

6 There are good reasons to assume that Nietzsche planned aphorisms BGE 231–9 as a separate chapter. Andreas Urs Sommer, in his detailed commentary of *Beyond Good and Evil*, confirms a letter to Carl Heymons and an earlier draft as indications that Nietzsche planned aphorisms 231–9 as a separate section with the title 'Das Weib an sich' (Sommer 2016: 652).

7 For the former, see Leiter (2013); Emden (2014); for the latter, see Reschke (2012); Oliver and Pearsall (1998).

8 On this transition, see Strauss (1983: 190).

9 The reference is to this text: 'Has my answer been heard to the question how one cures a woman – "redeems" her? One gives her a child. Woman needs children, a man is for her always only a means: thus spoke Zarathustra' (EH, 'Why I Write Such Good Books': 5).

10 Similar to Lynne Tirrell, for whom 'Nietzsche's misogyny is tempered by a surprising understanding of the situation of the (white, European, upper-class) women of his day' (Tirrell 1998: 219).

11 For another reading of Nietzsche as a misogynous despiser of women, see Klaas Meiler (2012). For a distinctly political reading, see David Owen (1998), who claims that Nietzsche's pronouncements on women may be read, on the one hand, 'as simply various aspects of a reactionary and contradictory essentialism' and, on the other hand, 'as masks manifesting an anti-essentialist pluralization and, indeed, dissolution of the category "woman"' (Owen 1998: 306). Both of these strategies of reading, Owen continues, exhibit a certain ontological politics: 'the former manifests itself as a legislative determination of the order of meaning, while the latter discloses itself as poetic dissolution of the possibility of a determinate semantic order' (ibid.), which correspond to the position of the philosopher as lawgiver and as poet respectively. Owen concludes: 'In considering the issue of a feminist politics it appears that Nietzsche's genealogical practice offers a notion of "strategic essentialism" which enables the construction of a specifically feminist politics around a concept of "woman" constituted through particular practical interests, while remaining open to otherness in that this concept of "woman" is a contingent construction' (ibid.: 320).

12 The discussion of the threat, for some, and the promise, from others, of androgyny in the late nineteenth century is a crucial feature of the socialisation

of sexuality, and will be discussed below. For this motif in Walter Benjamin's conception of the nineteenth century, see Greiert (2018).

13 For a critical discussion, in reference to Nietzsche, of a performative conception of gender as social role, see Paul Patton (2000). Although his critique is aimed at Judith Butler, it is unclear whether it does justice to Butler's point that the dualism of sex and gender along nature vs culture lines is precisely the problem. For a clear statement of this latter point, see Butler (1994, 1993), especially the essays 'Bodies that Matter' and 'Critically Queer'.

14 On this point, see also van Tongeren (2014: 159–61).

15 Heike Schotten (2018) has argued for an alliance between queer theory and Nietzsche based on the belief that 'morality is a political tool by which populations are segregated according to manufactured idealizations of merit or worth in order to stigmatize, demean, ostracize, and punish those deemed undeserving by its measure' (Schotten 2018: 5). However, Schotten does not relate Nietzsche's critique of morality to either probity or to sexuality, and thus the connection with queer theory remains purely at the level of 'method'.

16 Paul van Tongeren (2014) argues that the sections on 'das Weib an sich' provide an example of how Nietzsche envisages the 'cruel-probe thinking (grausam-redliche Denken)' of the philosopher beyond good and evil (van Tongeren 2014: 163). The text is inherently polemical in its tone, van Tongeren suggests, and as such offers a supreme example of Nietzsche's extra-moral and naturalised thought. Van Tongeren concludes with a warning that perhaps those who fail to see virtue in Nietzsche's apparently anti-feminist texts are those who misunderstand the basic problem 'man and woman' (BGE 238), who still wear the pigtail of our grandfathers (BGE 214) and whose virtue has become 'our limit, our stupidity (unsere Grenze, unsere Dummheit)' (BGE 227), a stupidity in which no god would hide but only an '"idea", a "modern idea"' (BGE 239) (van Tongeren 2014: 163–4).

17 Referring to the following citation: 'From the beginning, nothing has been more alien, repugnant, and hostile to woman than truth, – her great art is the lie, her highest concern is mere appearance (Schein) and beauty. Let us men confess it: we honour and love precisely this art and this instinct in woman (Weibe) . . .' (BGE 232).

18 On this point, see also Brusotti (2013).

19 See also Derrida (1979).

20 See also: 'There is not a woman, a truth in itself of woman in itself, that at least he has stated, and [through] the varied of typology, the crowd of

mothers, daughters, sisters, old maids, wives, governesses, prostitutes, virgins, grandmothers and granddaughters, of his work' (Derrida 1998: 63). For that very reason, there is no one truth of Nietzsche or of Nietzsche's text. For a somewhat unfair dismissal of Derrida's reading of truth and women, see Ansell-Pearson (1993).

21 See Ernst Bertram (2009) and his discussion of the problem of the actor and the question of '[w]hat forces create the Transformed Man?' According to Bertram, this question forms the core of *The Birth of Tragedy*: Dionysus is the name for the transformative power that forces people to become masks, masks of a super-personal, 'divine' being. *The Birth of Tragedy* reveals that 'the problem of transformation and of the enchantment of masks is still being seen and interpreted by an observer, not by someone who has himself been transformed; it is being experienced theoretically, *not* Dionysically' (Bertram 2009: 135). Nietzsche laments in his self-critical preface to have 'spoken' and not 'sung' about the power of transformation. The question of Nietzsche then becomes how to speak as a transformed human being, embodying the Dionysian, and not how to speak about the transformation of the human being, by enacting the Dionysian or playing the Dionysian man. Perhaps aphorisms 231–9 provide an example of Nietzsche's speaking from the place of transformation rather than about transformation.

22 See Foucault (1990b), who identifies the hysterisation of women through sexualisation as a means of biopolitical domination.

23 Sigridur Thorgeirsdottir (2012) argues that 'sexual differences are in many ways dependent on differences in biology and embodiment, but that does not mean that differences of the sexes constitute something like the "eternal feminine". Sexual differences are to no less extent determined by social and cultural contexts and conditions and thus change according to time and place. Nietzsche does in fact endorse changes in sexual differences. He is wary of a culture that has restricted women as sensual beings' (Thorgeirsdottir 2012: 69). On this point, see also the discussion of physical and spiritual pregnancy in Nietzsche by Skowron (2012). See also HH, 'Woman and Child' 377–437, GS Preface 3, 60, 339.

24 See also Laurence Lampert (2001), who distinguishes between two different conceptions of respect in the moderns and the ancients. He notes that in the opening Nietzsche speaks of the unusual attention (*Achtung*) now accorded to women, whereas at the end he speaks of a completely different respect (*Respekt*) accorded to women in Greek times, respect not based on the modern ideal of equality but on female

nature. According to Lampert, the difference between the two attitudes focuses on the passion of fear: 'women have reasonably lost their fear of modern man; Greek males reasonably feared women' (Lampert 2001: 239). I will further discuss the difference between the socialisation of sexuality in the moderns and in the ancients in the next section of this chapter.

25 See Freccero (2017) and her discussion of Derrida (2002), and Kofman (1984) on cats and Nietzsche.

26 'What Dante and Goethe believed about women – for the former when he sang, *"ella guarda suso, ed io lei"*, and the latter when he translated this, "the Eternal-Feminine attracts us higher" – I do not doubt that every nobler woman will resist this faith, for she believes the same thing about the Eternal-Masculine' (BGE 236).

27 See also Laurence Lampert (2001), who argues that Nietzsche's thinking about female–male relationships reflects nuances of the master–slave dialectic and as such cannot resolve the problem of domination: 'The nuances of a master–slave dialectic so prominent in everything Nietzsche says of female–male relations point to inescapable forms of slavery on both sides and achievable forms of mastery on both sides: beyond the primary male–female relationship, in the wider world for males; in the creation and formation of the child for females. If male mastery in the wider world extends to possession of females and a kind of mastery within the male–female relationship, the tension of that possession produces the cleverness and artfulness necessary for females to master the master' (Lampert 2001: 236).

28 For Riedel, this shift from a philosophy of living nature to a philosophy of the body, towards physiology, is nowhere more evident than in Nietzsche's philosophy of life: 'Body am I and soul [. . .] the soul is only a word for something in the body' (Z, 'On the Despisers of the Body').

29 Riedel notes, in line with Foucault, that the sexualisation of literary anthropology is not a consequence of psychoanalysis but, on the contrary, that psychoanalysis and the theory of drives stand with literary anthropology under the influence of the biological (and, I would add, biopolitical) conception of life as inherently sexual (Riedel 1996: XIV).

30 Like Marx, Nietzsche is critical of a paternalistic society that undermines the higher nature of women. According to Julian Young, Nietzsche fought hard to have women admitted to Basel University (Young 2010: 191, 390). Diethe and others have pointed out that some of his closest friends and associates were women, who exemplified and promoted the

cause of women, and so on. Also, in *Wanderer and his Shadow*, Nietzsche is critical of paternalist culture and society precisely because it disregards female intelligence (Diethe 1996: 287).

31 See Francis Nesbitt Oppel (2005: 36), on the idea that Nietzsche's thinking about feminine culture and feminine powers was influenced by Bachofen's theory of ancient matriarchy. On Nietzsche and Bachofen, see also Vatter (2015: 177–8).

Conclusion: Posthumanism and Community of Life

Throughout this book, I argue that for Friedrich Nietzsche the human being belongs entirely to nature and is an inseparable part of nature. In order to answer the question 'what is the human being?' Nietzsche disavows any teleological narrative and does not appeal to the transcendence of values that characterises metaphysical and religious approaches to the meaning of human life. For him, the human being has no essence because to be human is to be caught up in a dialectical movement such that the 'more natural' the human being attempts to become, the more it is able to 'overcome' itself. In the preceding chapters, I showed how this overhuman condition is for Nietzsche a cultural condition of artistic productivity and creativity that is attained by drawing from an experience of nature as chaos of drives and abyss of knowledge. This attainment is mediated by the cultivation of traits belonging to animal and plant life. By recognising the animality, and even plant-like being of the human, Nietzsche intimately links the attitude of scientific probity that discerns the continuum between nature and culture with an ethico-political conception of what is right by nature that is most closely approximated by the Cynics. For Nietzsche's free spirit or probe scientist, the question 'what is the human being?' is the same as the question 'what is natural to the human being?' or 'who is the natural human being?' Although, as shown above, Nietzsche works through the anti-natural humanism he associates with Christendom and draws from his interpretation of the Greeks as having come closest to developing the natural human being, the point of his teaching on *homo natura* is to show that no historical past of the human species formulates the correct answer to what is natural to the human being. The reason is that, for him, what comes naturally to the human is a capacity for transformation and metamorphosis of its way of being. According to the interpretation of *homo natura* in this book, Nietzsche's call to renaturalise the human species finally entails decentring its humanity with respect to the continuum of life that it is capable of embodying. In this sense, Nietzsche's teaching on *homo natura* signals the advent of posthumanism.

Two Forms of Posthumanism

As a critical discourse, contemporary posthumanism brings together all the key motifs already found in Nietzsche. A rejection of anthropomorphism and species hierarchy based on an idea of a continuum between nature and culture; a rejection of Kantian humanism in favour of a transformative, self-overcoming vision of the human; and, last but not least, a normative intent which seeks to redefine the possibility of an acting subject in contrast to a mere attribute of adaptation to given circumstances, without which posthumanism would cease to be a critical discourse (Braidotti 2016; Wolfe 2010). Yet, despite contemporary posthumanist discourse having a common precursor in Nietzsche's *homo natura*, posthumanism is also divided with respect to how it recovers its Nietzschean legacy of anti-humanism and anti-anthropomorphism. In this concluding section, I stage one possible representation of this division, which I shall describe in terms of the opposition between biopolitical and assemblage posthumanisms.

As examples of assemblage posthumanism, I shall take the work of Rosi Braidotti and Cary Wolfe. Despite the differences between the theoretical sources of their posthumanism – Gilles Deleuze for Braidotti, Jacques Derrida and Niklas Luhmann for Wolfe – they both understand posthumanism not so much as the 'erasure' of the human, but as a new description of 'the specificity of the human – its ways of being in the world, its ways of knowing, observing, and describing – by (paradoxically, for humanism) acknowledging that *it is fundamentally a prosthetic creature* that has coevolved with various forms of technicity and materiality, forms that are radically "not-human" and yet nevertheless made the human what it is' (Wolfe 2010: xxv).[1] Similarly, Braidotti says that posthumanism is the simultaneous embrace of two propositions (Braidotti 2010). The first one is found in Nietzsche as well: it states that there is no 'originary humanicity' (Kirby 2011). The second one, however, does not belong to Nietzsche: it states that there is only 'originary technicity' (MacKenzie 2006).

The second claim is fundamental to recent elaborations of technology-based transhumanism, such as is found in the narratives of Ray Kurzweil on Singularity and Yuval Harari on *Homo deus*.[2] The cybernetic and AI-driven posthumanism argues that technological progress will transform the human being into a superman or overman. By contrast, as I have shown in Chapter 1, Nietzsche's teaching on *homo natura* seeks to avoid any and all attempts to naturalise the human being through a reductive scienticism. Nietzsche avoids reductionism of this kind by offering a vision of scientific truth as probity, which entails affirming the unknowability of human nature, insofar as this draws from the chaotic and abyssal character of nature itself, and thereby the limits of human science. For Nietzsche, the overhuman condition is not attained by adding or supplementing technology to the human being, but instead by recognising the continuity of human experience with animal and plant life. It is only by drawing from this life, from what Ludwig Binswanger calls the 'inner history' of the lived embodiment, that the human being becomes creative.

The standpoint of biopolitical posthumanism, as developed out of Nietzsche's teaching on *homo natura*, understands technicity or technology as inherently immunitary. From this biopolitical perspective, and employing Giorgio Agamben's concept, there is no *anthropos* without an 'anthropological machine' that works by separating an originary community of life for which the distinction between *zoe* and *bios* is untenable, and recombining *zoe* and *bios* in an apparatus through which power is exercised over life (Agamben 2004). Biopolitical posthumanism, from this standpoint, turns on recovering a community of life beyond all attempts to immunise one species being against another. Biopolitical posthumanism articulates its anti-humanism and its anti-anthropormophism through an idea of common life rather than through the claim of the human originary prosthetic or assemblage being.

The difference between these two fundamental approaches to posthumanism can be appreciated by seeing the different role and function that animal and plant life receive in their self-understandings. For both Braidotti and Wolfe, there is a sense in which the animal question is opened only thanks to a cybernetic understanding of life as a self-productive, or autopoietic, system. In this sense, there would be no 'animal question' without a prior positing of the question of technology.[3] As Braidotti says:

> the distance one is likely to take from anthropocentrism *depends also on one's assessment of and relationship to contemporary technological developments*. In my work, I have always stressed the technophilic dimension and the liberating and even transgressive potential of these technologies. (Braidotti 2016: 16)[4]

For Braidotti, and the same applies to Wolfe's adoption of the Luhmannian idea of self-reference and self-closure of living systems, the continuum between nature and culture, the possibility of a community between human and non-human life, is ultimately based on what she terms 'the ubiquity of technological mediation' (ibid.: 17). The foundational claim of this assemblage posthumanism, according to which human nature is rejected in favour of 'the posthuman subject as a composite assemblage of human, non-organic, machinic and other elements' (ibid.: 19), is the transcendental fact of 'the structural presence of practices and apparati of mediation that inscribe technology as "second nature"' (ibid.).[5] In other words, and paradoxically, the human can enter into community with 'first nature' only by separating itself from it through technology as 'second nature'.

Neither Braidotti nor Wolfe thematise the interesting fact that the 'technical' or 'prosthetic' basis of their posthumanism is itself derivative from a variant of philosophical anthropology, namely, from Helmuth Plessner's interpretation of Nietzsche's *homo natura* in terms of an animal life that is radically incomplete and insecure, lacking in instinct, and whose being is from the start in need of compensation: a being who is 'artificial by nature' (Plessner 2003). Plessner draws the idea of the human being as a 'deficient' being from Nietzsche's critique of the human intellect as an insufficiently developed organ whose sole purpose is to compensate for the human being's relative weakness with respect to other animals and its environment (GS 110 and TL). In Nietzsche, the intellect is no longer the hallmark of the human being's superiority over nature and its technical advantage over animal life. But, in my account of *homo natura*, the insecurity of the human with respect to other forms of life is no longer the fundamental point of Nietzsche's philosophical anthropology. Rather, as discussed in Chapter 3 on the deconstruction of human nature through psychoanalysis, Nietzsche brings forth a discourse on the priority of the human body over the human soul as an organ of knowledge, while at the same time showing that it is the unknowability of drives that grants the transformative capacity of the human being. Nietzsche's philosophical anthropology starts from what Binswanger calls the 'inner history of life' rather than from the functionality of the human body. Whereas technicity always already seeks to enhance this functionality, it has little to say about the cultural self-transformation that engages the human being through its 'inner history' of the body. And, as discussed in the same chapter dedicated to psychoanalysis, for Nietzsche the roots of human creativity derive from the 'cruelty' of animality as much as from the drive to incorporation and reproduction characteristic of plant life: neither of these features denote for Nietzsche a source of weakness or powerlessness or insecurity. The presupposition of a human being in need of supplementary defence mechanism is itself internal to the immunitary logic of technology. As I show, Nietzsche (and Sigmund Freud) seek to overcome the so-called 'weakness' induced by the civilisational logic that erects barriers between human life (*bios*) and all other life (*zoe*) by calling for a recovery of nature as the ground of human creativity and self-overcoming. For Nietzsche, the problem of civilisation and technology is that they immunise the human being against its own animal and plant nature, separating the human being from the community of life and hence also from those drives and instincts that would otherwise allow it to meaningfully engage with other forms of non-human life.

Zoe-Egalitarianism and Community of Life

Deleuze's and Guattari's conception of anti-humanism as a function of 'becoming-animal' is clearly one of the most heavily Nietzsche-dependent conceptual constructions of the French philosophers (Deleuze and Guattari 1987). This Nietzschean element of Deleuze and Guattari is picked up by Braidotti's affirmation of 'zoe, or the generative force of non-human life' which 'rules through a trans-species and transgenic interconnection . . . which can best be described as an ecological philosophy of non-unitary embodied subjects and of multiple belongings' (Braidotti 2013: 203). In *The Posthuman*, Braidotti argues that the continuum between nature and culture entails a 'zoe-centered egalitarianism' (ibid.: 60).[6] By way of contrast, Wolfe rejects such egalitarianism because it would undermine the very idea of a self-referential auto-poietic system. There is, perhaps, no better way to clarify the difference between biopolitical and assemblage posthumanisms than by discussing the arguments for and against the possibility of *zoe*-egalitarianism.

The *zoe*-egalitarianism that Wolfe sets out to criticise in his *Before the Law* is the one espoused by Roberto Esposito and forms part of his proposed affirmative approach to biopolitics

(Wolfe 2013). Like Braidotti, Esposito also draws on Deleuze's idea of the becoming animal of the human being but, unlike Braidotti, he understands it through a discourse on community and immunity of life drawn from Nietzsche, and constructs from it what could be called a biopolitical posthumanism.

Esposito embraces two principles: first, the principle of biological continuity of life, and second, the unity and continuity of the totality of life where 'no part of it can be destroyed in favour of another: every life is a form of life and every form refers to a life' (Esposito 2008: 194). Wolfe speaks of the 'principle of unlimited equivalence for every single form of life' (Wolfe 2013: 56). Both principles are also at the heart of Nietzsche's conception of *homo natura* as I have argued throughout this book. For Esposito, as for Nietzsche, there is no hierarchy between forms of life, and all forms of life are to be affirmed indiscriminately. Whereas Esposito's affirmative biopolitics sees *zoe*-egalitarianism as contributing to the pluralisation of inherently singular forms of life, Wolfe advocates for a 'pragmatic' approach to determining which forms of life can be included in the human community of life and which ought to be excluded.

For Wolfe, there are certain forms of life (viral, for instance) that the human form of life must actively destroy if it is to survive. Wolfe objects to the 'unconditional embrace of all forms of life as subjects of immunitary protection' and instead recommends a return to a Derridean ethics of responsibility. He is of the view that all forms of life 'cannot be welcome, nor all at once' (ibid.: 103) and that a Derridean ethics of responsibility would provide us with the right tool to distinguish between those forms of life which fall under the protection of the law, and those which remain 'before the law' (ibid.: 103–5). However, it remains unclear how this pragmatic approach could prevent us from falling back into the distinction of the continuity of life into a hierarchy of species where some are valued more than others, where some are more welcome than others, where some are extinguished for the sake of the survival of others.

Unlike assemblage posthumanism and its prosthetic hypothesis, Esposito turns to Nietzsche and his conception of life in order to undo the human as a result of immunitary devices, or, in Agamben's terms, to break the 'anthropological machine' (Agamben 2004). In *Bios* Esposito (2008) identifies in Nietzsche both the expression of the self-destructive tendency found in the maximisation of immunity and what he calls 'hyperimmunity', and a more affirmative path in which immunity makes itself again the custodian and producer of life. On this view, the renaturalisation of the human being implies an opening up of the individual towards what is threatening to her in order to alleviate the grip that one's own self-protection has over the individual. Humans need to immunise themselves through a return to animality and break down all the artificial and spiritual illusions with which humans have sought to separate themselves for purposes of self-preservation from other living species. By breaking down the barriers of civilisation, humans would rediscover themselves as part of a community of life that affords human life among other forms of non-human life.

An affirmative biopolitics acknowledges that life as becoming continuously forms and transforms, creates and recreates itself in and through its multiple encounters with other forms of life. Life is creative, it gives itself a form and actively creates and recreates its various forms and ways of life. In this book, I have shown that these key features of life stand at the centre of Nietzsche's transformational conception of *homo natura*. Human nature mirrors life insofar as it is not only surplus, fullness and overabundance but also creativity, normativity and value creation. This is again an important point because it shows why an affirmative biopolitics contests the view that there exists a perspective outside and above life which 'gives' value, 'allows' life or 'assigns' the right to live, as Wolfe claims. Instead, life and value, life and norm, life and form are inseparable from each other to the extent that value, norm and form are inherent to life, expressions of the creativity of life.

Community of Life and Affirmative Biopolitics

Affirmative biopolitics has an important contribution to make to the debate on the inclusion and exclusion of life within the law. First, affirmative biopolitics provides an idea of politics that is oriented towards the becoming of community. Here, community stands for an experience of the common, where the latter does not designate a shared identity or common experience based on some sort of communal feeling of belonging that eliminates differences, but rather designates the communality of what is inherently plural and singular. From the perspective of affirmative biopolitics, community is possible only for what is different and plural, singular and 'impersonal', as Esposito puts it (2012). As such, affirmative biopolitics is not a politics of the 'subject of immunitary protection', as Wolfe (2013: 55) argues, but a politics of community that is a politics of 'pure relation', 'a relation without subjects' (Esposito 2008: 89).

Second, this striving for community comes hand in hand with a striving for justice. Justice does not refer to a reciprocal, contractual relationship between equals based on an economy of exchange, which is in the best interest of the two parties.

Instead, justice designates an asymmetrical relationship of gift-giving that is inherently a-economic and where what binds us to each other is the fact that we owe each other. We are bound to each other by an infinite responsibility to each other, an infinite debt that can never exhaust itself. It is in light of this debt that falls on us that we are equal. From the perspective of affirmative biopolitics, justice is based on gift-giving and expenditure. It is un-liberal and anti-utilitarian.

Up to here and in very general terms, this conception of community and justice is articulated by the new thinking of community in European philosophy, from Georges Bataille and Maurice Blanchot to Jean-Luc Nancy and Giorgio Agamben. What distinguishes these postmodern understandings of community is that the common bond is provided primarily by language, independently of whether by language we mean a given, spoken and lived practical idiom or whether by language we understand an ontological entity, language as the 'house of being', as in Martin Heidegger (2000).[7] By contrast, in affirmative biopolitics, the common bond is provided by a Nietzschean conception of life understood as a shared life that functions as the unifying force between different forms of life. Affirmative biopolitics thus offers a way to think together community and life. Nietzsche's teaching on *homo natura* brings to bear a new perspective on the current thinking about community by pointing out that human society is always preceded and exceeded by a community of life that is reflected in the human being's 'nature', the 'inner history' of its lived and embodied existence. Not language but shared life makes for genuine community. As discussed in relation to Freud's discovery of the human body, the histories of the human being are intermeshed with histories of animals and plants to the point of indistinction. The human

177

body is not a principle of closure and immunity that requires the defensive supplement of technicity, but is instead the place of shared life and connections with all forms of life, human and non-human. As exemplified by Nietzsche's understanding of the life of plants, including the human plant, the body does not have an identity closed onto itself separating between inner and outer, human and non-human forms of life. Rather, the human body as Nietzsche conceives it is embedded within an environment like a plant that is rooted in its soil, and hence connected to other forms of life.

Nietzsche's *homo natura* is thought as a form of life that is altered by its relationship to other forms of life on which it is deeply dependent. As such, *homo natura* affirms the totality of life and the radical interrelatedness between human and non-human forms of life. This idea of radical interrelatedness underpins affirmative biopolitics. In an affirmative biopolitics, politics no longer designates the realm of human affairs. Rather, as Esposito argues, drawing on Nietzsche's conception of will to power, it is life itself that is always already political.

Finally, my reading of *homo natura* suggests that there is a connection between Nietzsche's thinking about sexuality and the community of life. This would explain why 'Our Virtues', Chapter 7 of *Beyond Good and Evil*, ends with a discourse on sexuality and politics. This connection rests on the simultaneous discovery of sexuated reproduction of life at the heart of nineteenth-century conceptions of biological life, and sexual and familial relations as the basis of social reproduction. Given that according to Nietzsche, life is a pluralising and diversifying force, I argue that it is in the form of a sexual politics that the community of life expresses the politics of life inherent in it. On Nietzsche's account, it is through sexual differences that the politics of life alters and transforms settled juridical–political relations based on artificial conventions and social contracts. It is this anti-foundational relation between life and political power that leads Esposito after Nietzsche to contest the juridical–political categories of modern society, such as negative liberty and formal equality, as well as its self-legitimating discourse on the social contract, according to which political power is the result of free individuals who consent to a founding pact.

It is well known that so-called agonistic theories of democracy have contested the liberal pursuit of social order on the basis of an agreement that would bring peace and stability to the individual members by appealing to Nietzsche's conception of power, for which there is no final overcoming of struggle, contest and war, no final settling down into an ultimate equilibrium of life forces, but continuous, productive and open-ended conflict and contest. However, the political theory of agonism has not generally articulated Nietzsche's theory of will to power together with his affirmative politics of life based on an expanded community of life beyond the human. In the last chapter of this book, I argued that Nietzsche himself indicates the problem of sexuality and the 'basic problem of "man and woman"' as the decisive locus in which will to power and community of life come together. This articulation is reflected in Nietzsche's belief in the necessary antagonism between genders due to the non-existence of sexual nature. Against the fixation of human becoming on naturalised sexual difference, Nietzsche suggests viewing human sexuality as the ground for human transformation. Thus, I argued that Nietzsche employs sexuality in order to de-essentialise the human being. Following Derrida's reading, I showed that sexuality in Nietzsche denotes the alterity of human nature; an otherness in human nature that offers every individual the resources to withdraw and contest civilising discourses on moral and metaphysical truth that reflect forms of power over nature. But Nietzsche's discourse on sexuality and its unavoidable conflictuality and contestability also point towards Michel Foucault's rejection of sex as the 'hidden truth' of the human being and its connected employment of sexuality as an apparatus of power over life, as found in modern *scientia sexualis*. To these two interpretative standpoints, one needs to add Nietzsche's belief that conflict and contest can only be productive and fruitful when power relations reflect an equilibrium – there can be no contest between the weak and the strong, but always only between forces that are more or less equal. Here equilibrium and equality are the starting point of productive conflict that results in the constitution of a juridical order that does not settle into a final and absolute political form. From this point of view, it is the feminist egalitarian interpretation of Nietzsche's discourse on sexuality that has the last word, and the 'basic problem of "man and woman"' becomes the site for the construction of plural sexualities as non-dominating and transformational practice of being human.

Notes

1 Emphasis mine.
2 On the question of whether Nietzsche is a precursor or enemy of transhumanism, see Tuncel (2017).
3 Wolfe credits Luhmann, and Humberto Maturana and Francisco Varela for this cybernetic approach to life, but it is also of course found in Donna Haraway's ideal of the cyborg and then of the designed companion species, as exemplified by the Oncomouse and other such hybridisations or assembled life-forms (Haraway 2008). A similar idea is found also in the work of Katherine Hayles (1999), another precursor of contemporary posthumanist discourse.

4   Emphasis mine.

5   See also Braidotti (2013) where she asserts that 'boundaries between the categories of the natural and the cultural have been displaced and to a large extent blurred by the effects of scientific and technological advances' (Braidotti 2013: 3). For other statements on the technical basis of the 'nature-culture continuum', see ibid.: 61–2, 82–5, 103, 112, 136, 139, 158. In her article on the commonality between her standpoint and Haraway's, Braidotti (2006) speaks of a 'refusal to fall into the pitfall of the classical nature/culture divide: there is no natural telos or order, as distinct from technological mediation' (Braidotti 2006: 199).

6   Michiel van Ingen criticises this egalitarianism on the grounds that collapsing culture into nature does not allow for human agency, unless one believes that nature 'by itself' can resolve problems like climate change, etc. (van Ingen: 537).

7   The new thinking of community is in many ways a response to the crisis of humanism in the twentieth century. However, to date this thinking does not sufficiently problematise the vanishing frontier between human and non-human forms of life. One can distinguish two moments in the development of the debate on the crisis of humanism in the twentieth century. The first moment is exemplified by the 1940s exchange between Jean-Paul Sartre and Heidegger. It concerns the different receptions of Heidegger's early analytic of human existence (*Dasein*). In this first moment, the existence (*Dasein*) of the human being, in its manifold senses, is considered to be responsible for the de-centring of the human subject. The first moment of the debate in the crisis of humanism was followed by the 1960s structuralist and post-structuralist critiques of existentialism made by Claude Lévi-Strauss, Derrida and Foucault. It can be argued that this second moment of the debate results from the reception of the later Heidegger and his 'turn (*Kehre*)' away from the priority of human existence and towards the priority of language as the location of the possibility of ontology. According to this second debate on the crisis of humanism, what are de-centring the human subject are the linguistic, non-subjective structures of signification. On my hypothesis, the recent emergence of the animal theme in philosophy and in the humanities is symptomatic of a de-centring of the human subject that is new in comparison to the one found in the first and in the second debates on the crisis of humanism. Furthermore, this new development depends on a more recent reception of Nietzsche's philosophy, rather than the continuation of the reception of Heidegger's thought. Nietzsche's philosophy offers a

different perspective than Heidegger's on the crisis of humanism because Nietzsche understands human culture on the basis of the continuity between human and animal life forms. Heidegger's critique of humanism, on the contrary, maintains throughout the discontinuity between human and animal life forms. His critique of traditional humanism seeks, in effect, to propose a new humanism (Sloterdjik 1999). By contrast, Nietzsche's approach to culture, one which sees the constitution of meaning depend on the interaction with the animality of the human being rather than with its transcendence, opens new ways of thinking about a community of life between human and non-human forms of life.

Appendix

Friedrich Nietzsche (1989), *Beyond Good and Evil: Prelude to a Philosophy of the Future*, **trans. Walter Kaufmann, New York: Vintage Books. With minor amendments.**

Aphorism 230

What I have just said of a 'basic will of the spirit (*Grundwillen des Geistes*)' may not be readily understood: permit me an explanation. That commanding something which the people call 'the spirit' wants to be master in and around its own house and wants to feel that it is master; it has the will from multiplicity to simplicity, a will that ties up, tames, and is domineering and truly masterful. Its needs and capacities are so far the same as those which physiologists posit for everything that lives, grows, and multiplies. The spirit's power to appropriate the foreign stands revealed in its inclination to assimilate the new to the old, to simplify the manifold, and to overlook or repulse whatever is totally contradictory – just as it involuntarily emphasizes certain features and lines in what is foreign, in every piece of the 'external world', retouching and falsifying the whole to suit itself. Its intent in all this is to incorporate new 'experiences', to file new things in old files – growth, in a word – or, more precisely, the *feeling* of growth, the feeling of increased power.

An apparently opposite drive serves this same will: a suddenly erupting decision in favor of ignorance, of deliberate exclusion, a shutting of one's windows, an internal No to this or that thing, a refusal to let things approach, a kind of state of defense against that much that is knowable, a satisfaction with the dark, with the limiting horizon, a Yea and Amen to ignorance – all of which is necessary in proportion to a spirit's power to appropriate, its 'digestive capacity', to speak metaphorically – and actually 'the spirit' is relatively most similar to a stomach.

Here belongs also the occasional will of the spirit to let itself be deceived, perhaps with a capricious intimation of the fact that such and such is *not* the case, that one merely accepts such and such a delight in all uncertainty and ambiguity, a jubilant self-enjoyment in the arbitrary narrowness and secrecy of some nook, in the all too near, in the foreground, in what is enlarged, diminished, displaced, beautified, a self-enjoyment in the caprice of all these expressions of power.

Here belongs also, finally, that by no means unproblematic readiness of the spirit to deceive other spirits and to dissimulate in front of them, that continual urge and surge of a creative, form-giving, changeable force: in this the spirit enjoys the multiplicity and craftiness of its masks, it also enjoys the feeling of its security behind them: after all, it is surely its Protean arts that defend and conceal it best.

This will to mere appearance (*Schein*), to simplification, to masks, to cloaks, in short, to the surface – for every surface is a cloak – is *countered* by that sublime inclination of the seeker after knowledge (*Hang des Erkennenden*) who insists on profundity, multiplicity, and thoroughness, with a *will* which is a kind of cruelty (*Grausamkeit*) of the intellectual conscience and taste. Every courageous thinker will recognize this in himself, assuming only that, as fit, he has hardened and sharpened his eye for himself long enough and that he is used to severe discipline, as well as severe words. He will say: 'there is something cruel in the inclination of my spirit'; let the virtuous and kindly try to talk him out of that!

Indeed, it would sound nicer if we were said, whispered, reputed to be distinguished not by cruelty but by 'extravagant honesty', we free, *very* free spirits – and perhaps *that* will actually be our – posthumous reputation. Meanwhile – for there is plenty of time until then – we ourselves are probably least inclined to put on the garish finery of such moral word tinsels: our whole work so far makes us sick of this taste and its cheerful luxury. These are beautiful, glittering, jingling, festive words: honesty, love of truth, love of wisdom, sacrifice for knowledge, heroism of the truthful – they have something that swells one's pride. But we hermits and marmots have long persuaded ourselves in the full secrecy of a hermit's conscience that this worthy verbal pomp, too, belongs to the old mendacious pomp, junk, and gold dust of unconscious human vanity, and that under such flattering colors and make-up as well, the terrible basic text (*schreckliche Grundtext*) of *homo natura* must again be recognized.

To retranslate (*zurückübersetzen*) the human being back into nature; to become master over the many vain and overly enthusiastic interpretations and connotations that have so far been scrawled and painted over that eternal basic text (*Grundtext*) of *homo natura*; to see to it that the human being henceforth stands before man as even today, hardened in the discipline of science (*Zucht der Wissenschaft*), he stands before the *rest* (*anderen*) of nature, with intrepid Oedipus eyes and sealed Odysseus ears, deaf to the siren songs of old metaphysical bird catchers who have been piping at him all too long, 'you are more, you are

185

higher, you are of a different origin!' – that may be a strange and insane task (*seltsame und tolle Aufgabe*), but it is a *task* – who would deny that? Why did we choose this insane task? Or, putting it differently: 'why have knowledge at all? (*warum überhaupt Erkenntnis*)'

Everybody will ask us that. And we, pressed in this way, we who have put the same question to ourselves a hundred times, we have found and find no better answer—.

Friedrich Nietzsche (1968a), *The Antichrist*, trans. R. J. Hollingdale, London: Penguin Books. With minor amendments.

Aphorism 14

We have learned better (*umgelernt*). We have become more modest in every respect. We no longer trace the origin of the human being in the 'spirit', in the 'divinity', we have placed him back among (*zurückgestellt*) the animals. We consider him the strongest animal because he is the most cunning: his spirituality is a consequence of this. On the other hand, we guard ourselves against a vanity which would like to find expression even here: the vanity that the human being is the great secret objective of animal evolution. The human being is absolutely not the crown of creation: every creature stands beside him at the same stage perfection. . . . And even in asserting that we assert too much: the human being is, relatively speaking, the most unsuccessful (*missrathenste*) animal, the sickliest, the one most dangerously strayed from its instincts – with all that, to be sure, the most *interesting*! – As regards the animals, Descartes was the first who, with a boldness worthy of reverence, ventured to think of the animal as a *machine*: our whole science of

physiology is devoted to proving this proposition. Nor, logi-
cally, do we exclude the human being, as even Descartes did:
our knowledge of the human being today is real knowledge
precisely to the extent that it is knowledge of him as a machine.
Formerly the human being was presented with 'free will' as a
dowry from a higher order: today we have taken even will away
from him, in the sense that will may no longer be understood as
a faculty. The old word 'will' only serves to designate a resul-
tant, a kind of individual reaction which necessarily follows a
host of partly contradictory, partly congruous stimuli – the will
no longer 'effects' anything, no longer 'moves' anything. . . .
Formerly one saw in the human being's consciousness, in his
'spirit', the proof of his higher origin, his divinity; to make himself *perfect* the human being was advised to draw his senses back
into himself in the manner of the tortoise, to cease to have any
traffic with the earthly, to lay aside his mortal frame: then the
chief part of him would remain behind, 'pure spirit'. We have
thought better of this too: becoming-conscious, 'spirit', is to us
precisely a symptom of a relative imperfection of the organism,
as an attempting, fumbling, blundering, as a toiling in which
an unnecessarily large amount of nervous energy is expended –
we deny that anything can be made perfect so long as it is
still made conscious. 'Pure spirit' is pure stupidity: if we deduct
the nervous system and the senses, the 'mortal frame', *we miscalculate* – that's all! . . .

References

Abel, Günter (2001), 'Bewussten – Sprache – Natur. Nietzsches Philosophie des Geistes', *Nietzsche-Studien: Internationales Jahrbuch für die Nietzsche-Forschung*, 30: 1, pp. 1–43.

Acampora, Christa D. (2006), 'Naturalism and Nietzsche's Moral Psychology', in Keith Ansell-Pearson (ed.), *A Companion to Nietzsche*, Cambridge: Cambridge University Press, pp. 314–33.

Acampora, Christa D., and Keith Ansell-Pearson (2011), *Nietzsche's 'Beyond Good and Evil': A Reader's Guide*, London: Continuum.

Adorno, Theodor W., and Max Horkheimer (2002), *Dialectic of Enlightenment*, New York: Continuum.

Agamben, Giorgio (2004), *The Open: Man and Animal*, trans. K. Attell, Stanford: Stanford University Press.

Ansell-Pearson, Keith (1993), 'Nietzsche, Woman and Political Theory', in Paul Patton (ed.), *Nietzsche, Feminism and Political Theory*, London and New York: Routledge, pp. 27–48.

Ansell-Pearson, Keith (2000), 'On the Miscarriage of Life and the Future of the Human: Thinking beyond the Human Condition with Nietzsche', *Nietzsche-Studien: Internationales Jahrbuch für die Nietzsche-Forschung*, 29: 1, pp. 153–77.

Arendt, Hannah (1958), *The Human Condition*, Chicago: University of Chicago Press.

Assoun, Paul-Laurent (2000), *Freud and Nietzsche*, London and New York: Continuum.

Babich, Babette E. (2001), 'Nietzsche's Chaos Sive Natura: Evening Gold and the Dancing Star', *Revista Portuguesa de Filosofia*, 57, pp. 225–45.

Bachofen, Johann Jakob (1861), *Das Mutterrecht: Eine Untersuchung über die Gynaikokratie der Alten Welt nach ihrer religiösen und rechtlichen Natur*, Stuttgart: Verlag von Krais und Hoffmann.

Baeumler, Alfred (1928), 'Nietzsche und Bachofen', *Neue Schweizer Rundschau*, 5, pp. 323–43.

Bebel, August (1883), *Die Frau in der Vergangenheit, Gegenwart und Zukunft*, Zürich: Hottingen.

Becker, Gary S. (1996), *The Economic Way of Looking at Behaviour: The Nobel Lecture*, 69, Stanford: Hoover Institution Press.

Beekman, Tinneke (2009/2010), 'Turning Metaphysics into Psychology: Sigmund Freud and Friedrich Nietzsche', *New Nietzsche Studies*, 8: 1/2, pp. 98–118.

Benoit, Blaise (2012), 'Die Redlichkeit ("als Problem"): la vertu du philogue? Probité et justice selon Nietzsche', in Jean-François Balaud and Patrick Wotling (eds), *'L'art de bien lire': Nietzsche et la philologie*, Paris: Librairie Philosophique J. Vrin, pp. 95–107.

Bertino, Andrea Christian (2011a), '"As with Bees"? Notes on Instinct and Language in Nietzsche and Herder', in João Constâncio and Maria João Mayer Branco (eds), *Nietzsche on Instinct and Language*, Berlin and Boston: De Gruyter, pp. 3–34.

Bertino, Andrea Christian (2011b), *'Vernatürlichung'*, Berlin: De Gruyter.

Bertram, Ernst (2009), 'Mask', in *Nietzsche: Attempt at Mythology*, Urbana and Chicago: University of Illinois Press, pp. 134–53.

Binswanger, Ludwig (1947), *Ausgewählte Vorträge und Aufsätze, Band I. Zur phänomenologischen Anthropologie*, Bern: A. Francke.

Bishop, Paul (2009), 'Jung Looking at the Stars: Chaos, Cosmos and Archetype', *International Journal of Jungian Studies*, 1: 1, pp. 12–24.

Braidotti, Rosi (2006), 'Posthuman, All Too Human: Towards a New Process Ontology', *Theory, Culture and Society*, 23: 7–8, pp. 197–208.

Braidotti, Rosi (2013), *The Posthuman*, Cambridge and Malden, MA: Polity.

Braidotti, Rosi (2016), 'Posthuman Critical Theory', in Debashish Banerji and Makarand R. Paranjape (eds), *Critical Posthumanism and Planetary Futures*, New Delhi: Springer, pp. 13–36.

Branham, R. Bracht (1996), 'Defacing the Currency: Diogenes' Rhetoric and the Invention of Cynicism', in R. Bracht Branham and Marie-Odile Goulet-Cazé (eds), *The Cynics: The Cynic Movement in Antiquity and Its Legacy*, Berkeley, Los Angeles and London: University of California Press, pp. 81–104.

Brusotti, Marco (2011), 'Naturalismus? Perfektionismus? Nietzsche, die Genealogie und die Wissenschaften', in Marco Brusotti, Günter Abel and Helmut Heit (eds), *Nietzsches Wissenschaftsphilosophie: Hintergründe, Wirkungen und Aktualität*, Berlin and Boston: De Gruyter, pp. 59–91.

Brusotti, Marco (2013), 'Der schreckliche Grundtext Homo Natura: Texturen des Natürlichen im Aphorismus 230 von "*Jenseits von Gut und Böse*"', in Axel Pichler and Marcus Andreas Born (eds), *Texturen des Denkens: Nietzsches Inszenierung der Philosophie in 'Jenseits von Gut und Böse'*, Berlin and Boston: De Gruyter, pp. 259–78.

Brusotti, Marco (2014), 'Vergleichende Beschreibung versus Begründung. Das fünfte Hauptstück: "zur Naturgeschichte der Moral"', in Marcus Andreas Born (ed.), *Friedrich Nietzsche – Jenseits von Gut und Böse*, Berlin: Akademie Verlag, pp. 111–30.

Butler, Judith (1993), *Bodies that Matter: On the Discursive Limits of 'Sex'*, London: Routledge.

Butler, Judith (1994), 'Against Proper Objects', *Differences: A Journal of Feminist Cultural Studies*, 6: 2/3, pp. 1–26.

Butler, Judith (1999), *Gender Trouble*, New York: Routledge.

Clarke, Maudemarie (1998), 'Nietzsche's Misogyny', in Kelly Oliver and Marilyn Pearsall (eds), *Feminist Interpretations of Friedrich Nietzsche*, University Park: Pennsylvania State University Press, pp. 187–98.

Cohen, Alix A. (2008), 'Kant's Answer to the Question "What is Man?" and Its Implications for Anthropology', *Studies in History and Philosophy of Science*, 39, pp. 506–14.

Cox, Christoph (1999), *Nietzsche, Naturalism and Interpretation*, Berkeley, Los Angeles and London: University of California Press.

Deleuze, Gilles, and Félix Guattari (1987), *A Thousand Plateaus: Capitalism and Schizophrenia*, Minneapolis: University of Minnesota Press.

Derrida, Jacques (1979), *Spurs: Nietzsche's Styles/Éperons. Les styles de Nietzsche*, trans. B. Harlow, Chicago: University of Chicago Press.

Derrida, Jacques (1998), 'The Question of Style', in Kelly Oliver and Marilyn Pearsall (eds), *Feminist Interpretations of Friedrich Nietzsche*, University Park: Pennsylvania State University Press, pp. 50–80.

Derrida, Jacques (2002), *The Animal That Therefore I am*, New York: Fordham University Press.

Desmond, William (2008), *Cynics*, Berkeley, Los Angeles and London: University of California Press.

Diethe, Carol (1996), *Nietzsche's Women*, New York and Berlin: De Gruyter.

Emden, Christian J. (2014), *Nietzsche's Naturalism: Philosophy and the Life Sciences in the Nineteenth Century*, Cambridge: Cambridge University Press.

Esposito, Roberto (2008), *Bios: Biopolitics and Philosophy*, Minneapolis: University of Minnesota Press.

Esposito, Roberto (2011), *Immunitas: The Protection and Negation of Life*, trans. Z. Hanafi, Cambridge and Malden, MA: Polity.

Esposito, Roberto (2012), *Third Person: Politics of Life and Philosophy of the Impersonal*, trans. Z. Hanafi, Cambridge and Malden: Polity.

Firestone, Shulamith (2003), *The Dialectic of Sex: The Case for Feminist Revolution*, New York: Farrar, Straus and Giroux.

Fischer, Joachim (2018), '"Utopischer Standort" und "Urphantasie" des "noch nichr festgestellten Tieres". Nietzsche-Transformationen in der Philosophischen Anthropologie Plessners und Gehlens', in Thomas Ebke and Alexey Zhavoronkov (eds), *Nietzsche und die Anthropologie: Internationales Jahrbuch für Philosophische Anthropologie*, 7, Berlin and Boston: De Gruyter, pp. 153–72.

Foucault, Michel (1977), 'Nietzsche, Genealogy, History', in Donald F. Bouchard (ed.), *Language, Counter-Memory, Practice: Selected Essays and Interviews*, Ithaca: Cornell University Press, pp. 139–64.

Foucault, Michel (1990a), *The Archaeology of Knowledge*, London: Routledge.

Foucault, Michel (1990b), *The History of Sexuality*, trans. R. Hurley, vol. 1, New York: Vintage Books.

Foucault, Michel (1993), 'Dream, Imagination, and Existence', in Ludwig Binswanger and Michel Foucault, *Dream and Existence*, ed. Keith Hoeller, Atlantic Highlands, NJ: Humanities Press International, pp. 31–80.

Foucault, Michel (1994a), *Dits et Ecrits: 1954–1988*, vol. 1, Paris: Gallimard.

Foucault, Michel (1994b), *The Order of Things: An Archaeology of the Human Sciences*, New York: Vintage Books.

Foucault, Michel (1996), *Foucault Live: Interviews, 1961–1984*, ed. Sylvère Lotringer, New York: Semiotext(e).

Foucault, Michel (1997), 'Friendship as a Way of Life', in Michel Foucault, *Ethics: Subjectivity and Truth, Essential Works 1954–1984*, vol 1, ed. Paul Rabinow, New York: Vintage Books, pp. 135–40.

Foucault, Michel (2008), *Introduction to Kant's Anthropology*, Los Angeles: Semiotext(e).

Foucault, Michel (2010), *The Government of Self and Others: Lectures at the Collège de France, 1982–1983*, ed. Frédéric Gros, trans. G. Burchell, New York: Picador.

Foucault, Michel (2011), *The Courage of Truth (the Government of Self and Others II): Lectures at the Collège de France, 1983–1984*, trans. Burchell, Basingstoke and New York: Palgrave Macmillan.

Freccero, Carla (2017), 'Les chats de Derrida', in Christian Hite (ed.), *Derrida and Queer Theory*, Brooklyn: Punctum Books.

Freud, Sigmund (1933), *New Introductory Lectures on Psycho-analysis and Other Works*, trans. J. Strachey et al., *The Standard Edition of the Complete Psychological Works of Sigmund Freud*, vol. 22, London: The Hogarth Press.

Gasser, Reinhard (1997), *Nietzsche und Freud*, Berlin and New York: De Gruyter.

Gerhardt, Volker (2009), 'The Body, the Self and the Ego', in Keith Ansell-Pearson (ed.), *A Companion to Nietzsche*, Malden, MA: Blackwell, pp. 273–96.

Gillespie, Michael Allen (1999), 'Nietzsche and the Anthropology of Nihilism', *Nietzsche-Studien*, 28, pp. 141–55.

Gori, Pietro (2015), 'Nietzsche's Late Pragmatic Anthropology', *The Journal of Philosophical Research*, 40, pp. 377–404.

Goulet-Cazé, Marie-Odile (1996), 'Religion and the Early Cynics', in R. Bracht Branham and Marie-Odile Goulet-Cazé (eds), *The Cynics: The Cynic Movement in Antiquity and Its Legacy*, Berkeley, Los Angeles and London: University of California Press, pp. 47–80.

Goulet-Cazé, Marie-Odile (2014), *Cynicme et Christianisme dans l'antiquité*, Paris: Vrin.

Granier, Jean (1977), 'Nietzsche's Conception of Chaos', in David B. Allison (ed.), *The New Nietzsche*, Cambridge, MA: MIT Press, pp. 135–41.

Granier, Jean (1981), 'Le statut de la philosophie selon Nietzsche et Freud', *Revue de Métaphysique et de Morale*, 86: 1, pp. 88–102.

Greiert, Andreas (2018), '"Aufknacken der Naturteleologie", Androgynität und anthropologischer Materialismus bei Walter Benjamin', *Zeitschrift für kritische Theorie*, 46/47, pp. 74–95.

Ham, Jennifer (2004), 'Circe's Truth: On the Way to Animals and Women', in Christa D. Acampora and Ralph R. Acampora (eds), *A Nietzschean Bestiary: Becoming Animal Beyond Docile and Brutal*, Lanham: Rowman & Littlefield, pp. 193–210.

Han-Pile, Beatrice (2010), 'The "Death of Man": Foucault and Anti-Humanism', in Timothy O'Leary and Christopher Falzon (eds), *Foucault and Philosophy*, Oxford: Wiley-Blackwell, pp. 118–42.

Haraway, Donna J. (2008), *When Species Meet*, Minneapolis and London: University of Minnesota Press.

Harper, Kyle (2017), 'Freedom, Slavery, and Female Honor in Antiquity', in John Bodel and Walter Scheidel (eds), *On Human Bondage: After Slavery and Social Death*, Chichester: Wiley & Sons, pp. 109–21.

Harries, Karsten (1988), 'The Philosopher at Sea', in Michael Allen Gillespie and Tracy B. Strong (eds), *Nietzsche's New Seas: Explorations in Philosophy, Aesthetics, and Politics*, Chicago and London: University of Chicago Press, pp. 21–44.

Hatab, Lawrence J. (2015), 'Nietzsche, Nature, and the Affirmation of Life', in Vanessa Lemm (ed.), *Nietzsche and the Becoming of Life*, New York: Fordham University Press, pp. 32–48.

Hayles, Katherine (1999), *How We Became Posthuman: Virtual Bodies in Cybernetics, Literature and Informatics*, Chicago and London: University of Chicago Press.

Heidegger, Martin (2000), *Über den Humanismus*, Frankfurt: Vittorio Klostermann.

Heit, Helmut (2014), 'Erkenntniskritik und experimentelle Anthropologie. Das erste Hauptstück: "von den Vorurtheilen der Philosophen"', in Marcus Andreas Born (ed.), *Friedrich Nietzsche – Jenseits von Gut und Böse*, Berlin and Boston: De Gruyter, pp. 27–46.

Heit, Helmut (2016), 'Naturalizing Perspectives. On the Epistemology of Nietzsche's Experimental Naturalizations', *Nietzsche-Studien: Internationales Jahrbuch für die Nietzsche-Forschung*, 45: 1, pp. 56–80.

Higgins, Kathleen Marie (1998), 'Gender in *The Gay Science*', in Kelly Oliver and Marilyn Pearsall (eds), *Feminist Interpretations of Friedrich Nietzsche*, University Park: Pennsylvania State University Press, pp. 130–51.

Honenberger, Phillip (2016), 'Introduction', in Phillip Honenberger (ed.), *Naturalism and Philosophical Anthropology: Nature, Life, and the Human between Transcendental and Empirical Perspectives*, Basingstoke: Palgrave Macmillan, pp. 1–26.

Howey, Richard (1973), *Heidegger and Jaspers on Nietzsche: A Critical Examination of Heidegger's and Jaspers' Interpretations of Nietzsche*, The Hague: Martinus Nijhoff.

Irigaray, Luce (1991), *Marine Lover of Friedrich Nietzsche*, trans. G. C. Gill, New York: Columbia University Press.

Jaspers, Karl (1981), *Nietzsche: Einführung in das Verständnis seines Philosophierens*, Berlin: De Gruyter.

Jonas, Hans (2001), 'Is God a Mathematician? The Meaning of Metabolism', in Hans Jonas, *The Phenomenon of Life: Toward a Philosophical Biology*, Evanston, IL: Northwestern University Press, pp. 62–91.

Kant, Immanuel (1912), *Anthropologie; Fortschritte der Metaphysik/Vorlesungen Kants über Pädagogik/Vorlesungen Kants über Logik*, ed. Ernst Cassirer, 11 vols, vol. 8, *Immanuel Kants Werke*, Berlin: Bruno Cassirer.

Kant, Immanuel (2006), *Anthropology from a Pragmatic Point of View*, Cambridge: Cambridge University Press.

Kierkegaard, Soren (1962), *The Present Age*, New York: Harper and Row.

Kirby, Vicky (2011), *Quantum Anthropologies: Life at Large*, Durham, NC, and London: Duke University Press.

Klaas Meiler, Brigitta (2012), 'Frauen: Nur gut fürs Basislager oder auch für den philosophischen Höhenweg', in Renate Reschke (ed.), *Frauen: Ein Nietzschethema? Nietzsche: Ein Frauenthema?*, Berlin: Akademie Verlag, pp. 31–52.

Knobe, Joshua, and Brian Leiter (2007), 'The Case for Nietzschean Moral Psychology', in Brian Leiter and Neil Shinhababu (eds), *Nietzsche and Morality*, Oxford: Oxford University Press, 83–109.

Kofman, Sarah (1979), *Nietzsche et la scène philosophique*, Paris: Editions Galilée.

Kofman, Sarah (1983), *Nietzsche et la métaphore*, Paris: Editions Galilée.

Kofman, Sarah (1984), *Autobiogriffures: du chat Murr d'Hoffmann*, Paris: Editions Galilée.

Kofman, Sarah (1998), 'Baubô, Theological Perversion and Fetishism', in Kelly Oliver and Marilyn Pearsall (eds), *Feminist Interpretations of Friedrich Nietzsche*, University Park: Pennsylvania State University Press, pp. 21–49.

Krüger, Hans-Peter (2018), 'Von generöser Souveränität im europäischen Geist. Helmuth Plessners natur – und geschichtsphilosophische Kritik an Nietzsches Anthropo-Genealogie', in Thomas Ebke and Alexey Zhavoronkov (eds), *Nietzsche und die Anthropologie: Internationales Jahrbuch für Philosophische Anthropologie*, 7, Berlin and Boston: De Gruyter, pp. 137–52.

Lampert, Laurence (2001), *Nietzsche's Task: An Interpretation of Beyond Good and Evil*, New Haven and London: Yale University Press.

Large, Duncan (1990), '"Geschaffene Menschen": The Necessity of the Literary Self in Nietzsche, Musil and Proust', *Neohelicon*, 17: 2, pp. 43–60.

Leiter, Brian (1992), 'Nietzsche and Aestheticism', *Journal of the History of Philosophy*, 30: 2, pp. 275–90.

Leiter, Brian (2002), *Nietzsche: On Morality*, London: Routledge.

Leiter, Brian (2013), 'Nietzsche's Naturalism Reconsidered', in John Richardson and Ken Gemes (eds), *The Oxford Handbook of Nietzsche*, Oxford: Oxford University Press, pp. 579–98.

Lemm, Vanessa (2007), 'Is Nietzsche a Perfectionist? Rawls, Cavell and the Politics of Culture in Nietzsche's "Schopenhauer as Educator"', *Journal of Nietzsche Studies*, 34, pp. 5–27.

Lemm, Vanessa (2009), *Nietzsche's Animal Philosophy: Culture, Politics and the Animality of the Human Being*, New York: Fordham University Press.

Lemm, Vanessa (2013), 'Nietzsche, *Einverleibung* and the Politics of Immunity', *International Journal of Philosophical Studies*, 21: 1, pp. 3–19.

Lemm, Vanessa (2014a), 'The Embodiment of Truth and the Politics of Community: Michel Foucault and the Cynics', in Vanessa Lemm and Miguel Vatter (eds), *The Government of Life: Foucault, Biopolitics and Neoliberalism*, New York: Fordham University Press, pp. 208–23.

Lemm, Vanessa (ed.) (2014b), *Nietzsche y el devenir de la vida*, Santiago de Chile: Fondo de Cultura Económica.

Lemm, Vanessa (ed.) (2015), *Nietzsche and the Becoming of Life*, New York: Fordham University Press.

Lemm, Vanessa (2016a), 'Nietzsche and Biopolitics: Four Readings of Nietzsche as a Biopolitical Thinker', in Sergei Prozorow and Simona Rentea (eds), *The Routledge Handbook of Biopolitics*, London: Routledge, pp. 50–65.

Lemm, Vanessa (2016b), 'Is Nietzsche a Naturalist? Or How to Become a Responsible Plant', *Journal of Nietzsche Studies*, 47: 1, pp. 61–80.

Lemm, Vanessa (2018), 'Truth, Embodiment and Redlichkeit (Probity) in Nietzsche', in Manuel Dries (ed.), *Nietzsche on Consciousness and the Embodied Mind*, Berlin: De Gruyter Verlag 2018, pp. 289–307.

Lovejoy, Arthur O., and George Boas (1997), *Primitivism and Related Ideas in Antiquity*, Baltimore: Johns Hopkins University Press.

Löwith, Karl (1933), 'Kierkegaard und Nietzsche', *Deutsche Vierteljahrsschrift für Literaturwissenschaft und Geistesgeschichte*, 11, pp. 43–66.

MacKenzie, Adrian (2006), *Transductions: Bodies and Machines at Speed*, London: Continuum.

Marder, Michael (2013), *Plant-Thinking: A Philosophy of Vegetal Life*, New York: Columbia University Press.

Maurer, Reinhart (1990), 'Der andere Nietzsche. Zur Kritik der moralischen Utopie', *Deutsche Zeitschrift für Philosophie*, 38: 11, pp. 1019–26.

Meckel, Markus (1980), 'Der Weg Zarathustras als der Weg des Menschen. Zur Anthropologie Nietzsches im Kontext der Rede von Gott im "Zarathustra"', *Nietzsche-Studien*, 9, pp. 174–208.

Meinecke, Friedrich (1972), *Historism: The Rise of a New Historical Outlook*, New York: Herder & Herder.

Moles, John L. (1996), 'Cynic Cosmopolitanism', in R. Bracht Branham and Marie-Odile Goulet-Cazé (eds), *The Cynics: The Cynic Movement in Antiquity and Its Legacy*, Berkeley, Los Angeles and London: University of California Press, pp. 105–20.

Müller-Lauter, Wolfgang (1999), *Über Werden und Wille zur Macht: Nietzsche-Interpretationen I*, 3 vols, vol. 1, Berlin: De Gruyter.

Nancy, Jean-Luc (1990), '"Our Probity!" On Truth and Lie in the Moral Sense in Nietzsche', in Laurence A. Rickels (ed.), *Looking After Nietzsche*, Albany: State University of New York Press, pp. 67–87.

Navia, Luis E. (2005), *Diogenes the Cynic: The War against the World*, Amherst, MA: Humanity Books.

Nehamas, Alexander (1987), *Nietzsche: Life as Literature*, Cambridge, MA: Harvard University Press.

Nesbitt Oppel, Francis (2005), *Nietzsche on Gender: Beyond Man and Women*, Charlottesville: University of Virginia Press.

Niehus-Pröbsting, Heinrich (1988), *Der Kynismus des Diogenes und der Begriff des Zynismus*, Frankfurt: Suhrkamp.

Nietzsche, Friedrich (1968a), *The Antichrist*, trans. R. J. Hollingdale, London: Penguin Books.

Nietzsche, Friedrich (1968b), *Twilight of the Idols*, trans. R. J. Hollingdale, London: Penguin Books.

Nietzsche, Friedrich (1986), *Human, All Too Human*, trans. R. J. Hollingdale, Cambridge: Cambridge University Press.

Nietzsche, Friedrich (1988), *Sämtliche Werke*, Kritische Studienausgabe in 15 Bänden, ed. Giorgio Colli and Mazzino Montinari, Berlin: De Gruyter.

Nietzsche, Friedrich (1989), *Beyond Good and Evil: Prelude to a Philosophy of the Future*, trans. W. Kaufmann, New York: Vintage Books.

Nietzsche, Friedrich (1990), *Twilight of the Idols and Anti-Christ*, trans. R. J. Hollingdale, London: Penguin.

Nietzsche, Friedrich (1994), *On the Genealogy of Morals*, trans. C. Diethe, Cambridge: Cambridge University Press.

Nietzsche, Friedrich (1995), *Thus Spoke Zarathustra*, trans. W. Kaufmann, New York: Modern Library.

Nietzsche, Friedrich (1997a), *Daybreak*, trans. R. J. Hollingdale, Cambridge: Cambridge University Press.

Nietzsche, Friedrich (1997b), *Untimely Meditations*, trans. R. J. Hollingdale, Cambridge: Cambridge University Press.

Nietzsche, Friedrich (1997c), 'Homer's Contest', in Friedrich Nietzsche, *On the Genealogy of Morality*, trans. C. Diethe, Cambridge: Cambridge University Press, pp. 174–81.

Nietzsche, Friedrich (1999), *The Birth of Tragedy*, trans. R. Speirs, Cambridge: Cambridge University Press.

Nietzsche, Friedrich (2001), *The Gay Science*, trans. J. Nauckoff, Cambridge: Cambridge University Press.

Oliver, Kelly (1998), 'Women as Truth in Nietzsche's Writing', in Kelly Oliver and Marilyn Pearsall (eds), *Feminist Interpretations of Friedrich Nietzsche*, University Park: Pennsylvania State University Press, pp. 66–80.

Oliver, Kelly, and Marilyn Pearsall (eds) (1998), *Feminist Interpretations of Friedrich Nietzsche*, University Park: Pennsylvania State University Press.

Orsucci, Andrea (1996), 'Orient – Okzident: Nietzsches Versuch einer Loslösung vom europäischen Weltbild', *Monographien und Texte Zur Nietzsche-Forschung*, Berlin and New York: De Gruyter.

Owen, David (1998), 'Nietzsche's Squandered Seductions: Feminism, the Body, and the Politics of Genealogy', in Kelly Oliver and Marilyn Pearsall (eds), *Feminist Interpretations of Friedrich Nietzsche*, University Park: Pennsylvania State University Press, pp. 306–26.

Patterson, Orlando (2017), 'Revisiting Slavery, Property, and Social Death', in John Bodel and Walter Scheidel (eds), *On Human Bondage: After Slavery and Social Death*, Chichester: Wiley & Sons, pp. 265–96.

Patton, Paul (2000), 'Nietzsche and the Problem of the Actor', in Alan D. Schrift (ed.), *Why Nietzsche Still?*, Berkeley: University of California Press, pp. 170–83.

Pieper, Annemarie (1990), *'Ein Seil geknüpft zwischen Tier und Übermensch': Philosophische Erläuterungen zu Nietzsches erstem 'Zarathustra'*, Stuttgart: Klett-Cotta.

Pieper, Annemarie (2012), 'Nietzsche und die Geschlechterfrage', in Renate Reschke (ed.), *Nietzscheforschung: Frauen: Ein Nietzschethema? – Nietzsche: Ein Frauenthema?: Jahrbuch der Nietzschegesellschaft: 19*, Berlin: De Gruyter, pp. 53–63.

Plessner, Helmuth (2003), *Die Stufen des Organischen und der Mensch. Einleitung in die philosophische Anthropologie*, Frankfurt: Suhrkamp Verlag.

Reschke, Renate (ed.) (2012), *Nietzscheforschung: Frauen: Ein Nietzschethema? – Nietzsche: Ein Frauenthema?: Jahrbuch der Nietzschegesellschaft: 19*, Berlin: De Gruyter.

Richardson, John (2009), *Nietzsche's New Darwinism*, Oxford: Oxford University Press.

Riedel, Wolfgang (1996), *'Homo Natura': Literarische Anthropologie um 1900. Quellen und Forschungen zur Literatur- und Kulturgeschichte*, Berlin and New York: De Gruyter.

Rogers, Susan Carol (1978), 'Women's Place: A Critique of Anthropological Theory', *Comparative Studies in Society and History*, 20: 1, pp. 123–62.

Rubin, Gayle (1975), 'The Traffic of Women: Notes on the Political Economy of Sex', in Rayna R. Reiter (ed.), *Towards an Anthropology of Women*, New York: Monthly Review Press, pp. 157–210.

Sanford, Whitney, and Vandana Shiva (eds) (2012), *Growing Stories from India: Religion and the Fate of Agriculture*, Lexington: University Press of Kentucky.

Santini, Carlotta (2020), 'Zwischen Geschichte und Gedächtnis. Aby Warburg, Jacob Burckhardt und Friedrich Nietzsche', in Anthony K. Jensen and Carlotta Santini (eds), *The Re-encountered Shadow: Nietzsche on Memory and History*, New York and Berlin: De Gruyter.

Schacht, Richard (1995), *Making Sense of Nietzsche*, Urbana and Chicago: University of Illinois Press.

Schacht, Richard (2006), 'Nietzsche and Philosophical Anthropology', in Keith Ansell-Pearson (ed.), *A Companion to Nietzsche*, Malden, MA: Blackwell, pp. 115–32.

Schlossberger, Matthias (1998), 'Über Nietzsche und die Philosophische Anthropologie', *Nietzscheforschung*, 4, pp. 147–67.

Schotten, Heike C. (2018), 'Nietzsche and Emancipatory Politics: Queer Theory as Anti-Morality', *Critical Sociology*, 45: 2, pp. 213–26.

Schrift, Alan D. (2001), 'Rethinking the Subject: Or How One Becomes-Other Than What One Is', in Richard Schacht (ed.), *Nietzsche's Postmoralism: Essays on Nietzsche's Prelude to Philosophy's Future*, Cambridge: Cambridge University Press, pp. 47–62.

Siemens, Herman (2015), 'Nietzsche's Conception of "Necessity" and Its Relation to "Laws of Nature"', in Vanessa Lemm (ed.), *Nietzsche and the Becoming of Life*, New York: Fordham University Press, pp. 82–104.

Skowron, Michael (2012), '"Schwanger geht die Menschheit" (*Nachgelassene Fragmente* 1882/83): Friedrich Nietzsches Philosophie des Leides und der Zukunft', in Renate Reschke (ed.), *Nietzscheforschung: Frauen: Ein Nietzschethema? – Nietzsche: Ein Frauenthema?: Jahrbuch der Nietzschegesellschaft: 19*, Berlin: De Gruyter, pp. 223–44.

Sloterdijk, Peter (1983), *Kritik der zynischen Vernuft*, Frankfurt: Suhrkamp.

Sloterdijk, Peter (1999), *Regeln für den Menschenpark. Ein Antwortschreiben zu Heideggers Brief über den Humanismus*, Frankfurt: Suhrkamp.

Sommer, Andreas Urs (2016), *Kommentar zu Nietzsches Jenseits von Gut und Böse*, Berlin and Boston: De Gruyter.

Stegmaier, Werner, and Andrea Bertino (2015), 'Nietzsches Anthropologiekritik', in Marc Rölli (ed.), *Fines Hominis?: Zur Geschichte der philosophischen Anthropologiekritik*, Bielefeld: Transcript Verlag, pp. 65–80.

Strauss, Leo (1983), *Studies in Platonic Political Philosophy*, Chicago: University of Chicago Press.

Strauss, Leo (1995), *Philosophy and Law: Contributions to the Understanding of Maimonides and his Predecessors*, New York: State University of New York Press.

Strong, Tracy B. (2015), 'The Optics of Science, Art, and Life: How Tragedy Begins', in Vanessa Lemm (ed.), *Nietzsche and the Becoming of Life*, New York: Fordham University Press, pp. 19–31.

Thorgeirsdottir, Sigridur (2012), 'Baubô: Laughter, Eroticism and Science to Come', in Renate Reschke (ed.), *Nietzscheforschung: Frauen: Ein Nietzschethema? – Nietzsche: Ein Frauenthema?: Jahrbuch der Nietzschegesellschaft: 19*, Berlin: De Gruyter, pp. 65–73.

Tirrell, Lynne (1998), 'Sexual Dualism and Women's Self-Creation: On the Advantages and Disadvantages of Reading Nietzsche for Feminists', in Kelly Oliver and Marilyn Pearsall (eds), *Feminist Interpretations of Friedrich Nietzsche*, University Park: Pennsylvania State University Press, pp. 199–224.

Tocqueville, Alexis de (2003), *Democracy in America and Two Essays on America*, London: Penguin.

Tuncel, Yunus (ed.) (2017), *Nietzsche and Transhumanism: Precursor or Enemy*, Cambridge: Cambridge Scholars.

van Ingen, Michiel (2016), 'Beyond the Nature/Culture Divide? The Contradictions of Rosi Braidotti's *The Posthuman*', *Journal of Critical Realism*, 15: 5, pp. 530–42.

van Tongeren, Paul (2014), '"Nietzsches Redlichkeit." Das Siebte Hauptstück: "Unsere Tugenden"', in Marcus Andreas Born (ed.), *Friedrich Nietzsche – Jenseits von Gut und Böse*, Berlin and Boston: De Gruyter, pp. 147–66.

Vatter, Miguel (2015), *The Republic of the Living*, New York: Fordham University Press.

Visser, Gerard (1999), 'Nietzsches Übermensch. Die Notwendigkeit einer Neubesinnung auf die Frage nach dem Menschen', *Nietzsche-Studien*, 28, pp. 100–24.

White, Alan (2001), 'The Youngest Virtue', in Richard Schacht (ed.), *Nietzsche's Postmoralism: Essays on Nietzsche's Prelude to Philosophy's Future*, Cambridge: Cambridge University Press, pp. 63–78.

Whyte, Max (2008), 'The Uses and Abuses of Nietzsche in the Third Reich: Alfred Baeumler's "Heroic Realism"', *Journal of Contemporary History*, 43: 2, pp. 171–94.

Wolfe, Cary (2010), *What is Posthumanism?*, Minneapolis: University of Minnesota Press.

Wolfe, Cary (2013), *Before the Law: Humans and Other Animals in a Biopolitical Frame*, Chicago and London: University of Chicago Press.

Wotling, Patrick (1995), *Nietzsche et le problème de la civilisation*, Paris: Presses universitaires de France.

Wotling, Patrick (2008), *La philosophie de l'esprit libre: Introduction à Nietzsche*, Paris: Flammarion.

Young, Julian (2010), *Friedrich Nietzsche: A Philosophical Biography*, Cambridge: Cambridge University Press.

Index

aestheticism, negative thesis of, 19–20
agonism, theory of, 179
animal life
the animal as machine, 87–8
in assemblage posthumanism, 170–1
becoming-animal, 173
cruelty and cultural production, 7, 33–4, 51–3, 60–1, 130, 172
in Cynicism, 33
of the human being, 51–5, 85–8, 130–1
and the overcoming of the human, 94–6, 102, 167
the renaturalisation of the human to, 86–91
sickness of the human animal, 85–6
study of in literary anthropology, 44, 55
study of in philosophical anthropology, 44, 51
anthropology
and the body, 105n, 106n
Foucault's critique of, 5, 13, 14–15, 21, 74–5
illusion of human knowledge, 14–16, 21
see also philosophical anthropology
The Antichrist 14 aphorism
critique of civilisation in, 77, 83–6
deconstruction of the human, 86–8
full text of, 186–7
naturalism imperative, 3, 20, 72
sickness of the human animal, 85–6
anti-humanism, 11, 51, 169, 170, 173
Arendt, Hannah, 50, 148
art
as the creation of society, 160–1
dependence-relation between art and nature, 104n
nature as, 8, 57–8

Bachofen, Johann Jakob, 9, 125, 155, 158
Baeumler, Alfred, 125